Cor...
Change
Required

Becoming Who You
Really Want to Be

By
Bill Epperhart

Correct Change Required

Correct Change Required by Bill Epperhart
Published by Insight Publishing Group
8801 S. Yale, Suite 410
Tulsa, OK 74137
918-493-1718

Unless otherwise noted, all Scripture quotations are from the New King James version of the Bible, copyright © 1979, 1980, 1982, by Thomas Nelson, Inc., publishers.

Cover design by Jeffrey Mobley

ISBN 1-930027-21-4
Library of Congress catalog card number: 00-104489

Printed in the United States of America

Dedication

I dedicate this book to my loving wife of twenty-five years, Becky, and to my children, Brooke and Brant. Without their constant love and support, none of this would have been possible.

Acknowledgments

I would like to recognize several people who helped me with this book.

I am thankful for divine connections with men who have guided me at critical junctures in my life. I appreciate so much B.B. Hankins, Bill Behrman, Cecil Janway, and David Briggs.

The editorial work is a process of change itself! I want to thank my secretary, Lynn Shotwell, for the oversight of this process. Laura Black and Claudia Henning spent many hours transcribing the material in preparation for editing. Kim Ramos did a wonderful job editing and writing.

I want to thank my church family, staff, and board for their support and faithfulness.

To all of you I give my utmost appreciation for a job well done. Because of you, many people will share in this process of change that has brought us much success!

Contents

Foreword

By John Mason

I often tell people not to be like cement, all mixed up and permanently set. Be proactive and take the initiative to change and improve. When unexpected changes force themselves on you, use them to your advantage. Use change to improve yourself, to become more than mediocre. I strongly believe in the message that Bill Epperhart shares in this book, *Correct Change Required*.

He explains the stages of change and the transformation that can take place within when you overcome the influences of the past and the strongholds that keep you back. After all, the one thing that remains the same is change itself. So don't fear change; embrace it.

Take his words to heart as he encourages you and pushes you on toward growth. No obstacle will ever leave you the way it found you; may you learn to let the influences of change make you stronger, not make you stagger. I believe that God will use this book to help people grow and become all that God wants them to be.

Introduction

Change cannot be described as a gentleman. It never knocks on your door but barges its way into your life. Most people experience change due to external events—events that happen around them. After ten years of marriage, a husband announces he is leaving; an executive loses his position after a company merger; a mother of several preschool children is diagnosed with a terminal illness. Change forces itself upon us in various and unusual ways. Many times we end up feeling like victims of our circumstances.

This is not the way God intended for us to live. We are created in the image of God, and like Him we have the power to choose. We do not have to sit around, waiting for change to strike. We can choose to change. With a little introspection and foresight, we can stay ahead of the game of life. We can evaluate whether or not the direction we are heading will take us to the place we want to go. If not, we can change our course midstream. We have a lot more control than we think we do.

What hinders most people from taking that control is a lack of knowledge. They want to change, but they do not know how. They do not understand the process of change; they have no clue about its various stages, and they do not know how it works. The purpose of this book is to equip you to change. Understanding change gives you an edge when dealing with it. Understanding arms you for follow-through. Being able to identify where you are in the stages of change keeps you from getting discouraged. You see the light at the end of the tunnel, and you know you can make it.

Choosing to make needed changes in your life and following through with those changes is a godlike task. You must strike the circumstances before they strike you! You create something new with your choices. You go against the tide and begin to swim upstream toward a destiny of your own desire. Even after taking on an aggressive mentality like this, you are still going to be faced with negative experiences. There are still going to be circumstances that try to destroy you, circumstances for which you are ill prepared.

There is still something you can do.

Even when change forces itself upon you in a horrendous way, there is still a decision to be made. You may have no control over the circumstance. It may catch you totally off guard. It may rush in like a flood, trying to destroy everything in the path of your life, but you still have a choice.

You can still choose your response.

No matter how tragic the circumstances, no matter how unexpected the events, you still have the power to choose your response to any change. It is not something that is easy; it is not something that is natural. But it is possible. It is the only sure way of overcoming a victim's mentality. It is your only hope of staying on track.

Choosing your response is something that must be learned. You can equip yourself to deal with any change, but it takes practice. You practice by making proactive changes—changes no one is forcing you to make. By initiating changes in your life and following through with those changes, you learn the art of change. You learn its process. Then, when forced change shows up on your doorstep and hits you squarely on the head, you are equipped. You know how to deal with it. You have already put yourself through boot camp, and you are ready for war.

Change is a spiritual battle, but we possess mighty weapons of war. The Bible gives us specific strategies for making proactive changes and for dealing with forced change when it comes. The information found in the Bible is obviously spiritual, reaching the deepest parts of the heart, but it is intensely practical as well. The Bible outlines the process of change and also teaches us the practical steps we need to take to make sure those changes happen.

Jesus was the Change Master. Everywhere He went He was proactive. He always ministered change—significant, positive change: when He turned the water into wine, when He healed the blind man, and when He touched the leper and made him clean.

Jesus always changed lives for the better. It is exciting to know that He wants to bring positive changes into our lives as well.

Jesus also had to deal with forced change. He suffered at Golgotha and had to choose His response. Under the most tragic of circumstances, His right response carried Him through, and ultimately He had victory, even out of the depths of horror, even out of the belly of the grave.

Thoreau made the observation, "Most people lead lives of quiet desperation." In other words, in their heart of hearts people are always looking for change. They want their circumstances to be different. They are always looking to improve their lives. Most of the time, however, they do not know where to start. Life continues drifting by them.

You are either growing or decaying, but you are constantly changing. In five years, you will have changed. The question is how. In five years, you will be somewhere. The question is where. In five years, you will be someone different. The question is who. It is up to you. The major key to a better future is you. You can be proactive and choose to make needed changes in your life, or you can let yourself drift along until circumstances force you to change.

What is it about your life that you would like to change? Would you like to have stronger relationships with other people? Would you like your finances to increase? Would you like to feel better about yourself and others? Would you like to enjoy greater success? If you want to change in any way, this book is for you. The purpose of this material is to help you understand the process of change so that you can develop strategies that will make you successful in that process. You can experience positive, permanent change in your life. You can change!

1
Preparing for Personal Change

Every change begins with an ending. Something in your life has to die before real change can take place. I finally realized that there were certain foods I had to eliminate from my diet. Rice and gravy were two of them. I had to have a funeral for rice and gravy; I had to bury them because they were making me fat!

To actually lay hold of the changes you need to make in your life, you must let go of the status quo. You simply cannot continue to do things the same way you have always done them! If, like me, your desire is to lose weight, you have to adopt new beliefs about food. Your behavior must also change. You cannot continue eating Big Macs for dinner every night. That may feel like a real loss to you. People do not resist change; they resist the loss associated with it.

The caterpillar has to die before it can be transformed into a butterfly. Likewise, we must die to our old ways before we can be transformed into something new. For an alcoholic to stop drinking, he has to die to alcohol. This is a scriptural principle. The Bible teaches us to "reckon" ourselves dead to sin—to consider ourselves dead to the harmful behaviors in our lives (Romans 6:11).

Reckoning yourself dead to sin is not easy, but death is never pleasant! This death is necessary, however, if new life is to begin. Jesus said that unless a grain of wheat falls into the ground and dies, it cannot produce anything (John 12:24). If you do not die to the destructive things in your life, you will not be able to flourish and produce fruit at a new level. To prepare yourself for change, you must understand that dying to the old is a vital step toward embracing the new.

....

What Do You Want To Change?

Another way to prepare yourself for successful transformation is to specifically identify the things you want to change. You need to ask yourself, "What exactly is it that I want?" In Mark 11, Jesus instructs us to identify in prayer the things we desire. You need to know what you desire. Most people just drift through life without ever knowing what it is that they really want.

Not far from my house is a launching pad for hot air balloons. Those big, colorful balloons are magnificent against the backdrop of the Colorado sky, but the pilots can never be quite sure of where the balloons will land. Several balloons have actually touched down in my backyard! A pilot can control the elevation of the balloon, but he or she is totally at the mercy of the wind.

Just like these hot air balloons, many people rise up and get excited about the possibility of change, but because they never identify their specific desires, they end up drifting along and landing at an unforeseen destination. They may be aware of a few things that they do not like about their lives, issues that make them uncomfortable, but they cannot define what they want to see changed. They know that they want the problem to go away, but they cannot tell you much more than that. They may even have some fuzzy dreams or a few vague goals, but because these are not clearly defined, their lives just continue to drift off course.

James Goddard is a great example of someone who refused to drift along in life. As a teenager, he wrote down 127 specific things he wanted to accomplish. He included goals he would like to accomplish, places he would like to go, people he would like to meet, and the type of person he would like to become. Those goals included milking a rattlesnake, reading the entire *Encyclopaedia Britannica*, and climbing to the top of Mt. Everest! In the last report I heard, he had accomplished the majority of those goals. He was able to accomplish them because he had first *identified* them.

To identify what you want to change in your life, it is helpful to imagine the rest of your life as a book with blank pages. Now picture yourself writing how the book will end. God gave us the right to compose the ending of our own book when He gave us the power to choose. He makes this very clear in Deuteronomy 30 when He tells us to "choose life."

What would you like to do? What would you like to become? What would you like to accomplish? Whom would you like to meet? Where would you like to go? Define *exactly* what you want, or change will never happen!

Areas in Need of Change

All the major areas of your life can be improved with change. It may be helpful to think about each area and define what you want. It is a very good idea to write these wants in a journal or in a permanent notebook. Seeing them on paper will solidify them as goals.

Area #1: Spiritual and Ethical Life

You can grow and change so that your spirit becomes stronger. My prayer life, for example, was revolutionized when a friend mentored me in this area. Other avenues of spiritual growth may be reading and studying your Bible, being honest in the little things, or even working toward discovering your primary purpose in life.

Area #2: Family and Home

It seems that almost everyone has issues of forgiveness. We all have fences to mend with a relative, a spouse, a child, or a neighbor. You may argue, "But you just don't understand! That person is impossible!" I do understand; I have relatives myself, but I also understand how important it is for you to let go of any bitterness. You have to protect your heart from it, or it will absolutely destroy you. You cannot control how your relatives are, but you can control how you are.

You can also define the positive things you want in your relationships. I write down goals for what I want to see happen with my wife and kids—one-year, three-year, five-year, and ten-year goals. You may think that is a little compulsive, but I guarantee you my family is not neglected. I never take my family for granted because my goals keep me accountable.

Another aspect of the family and home area is improving practical things, such as installing new carpet in your house or purchasing a hot tub. Every year between Christmas and New Year's Day I categorize goals like this in my journal.

Area #3: Financial and Career Life

Do you have career goals? Perhaps there are changes looming on the horizon in this area. You need to come up with a plan! What would you really like to do? Maybe you want to change your finances; it is never too late to learn how to save and invest. You need to set goals to make your income increase and to continue developing your skills for the marketplace.

Area #4: Mental and Educational Life

Some of you need to go back to school. You may want to learn a foreign language or become computer literate. Others need to commit to more independent study. To continue growing mentally, you should read at least a book a week. If you do not, in ten years you will be more than five hundred books behind! There are many opportunities for growth in this area; it all depends on your personal goals.

Area #5: Physical Life and Health

Proper weight, exercise, and blood pressure are obviously important factors in your life. If you are not concerned about these things, you should be. If your health deteriorates, how can you enjoy what you accomplish in any of these other areas?

Area #6: Social Life and Relationships

Set goals for your relationships. Write down what you desire. Maybe you need some new friends, ones who will encourage you to keep growing and changing. How will you meet them? Maybe you need to change something about your marriage relationship or need to spend more time with your children.

Identifying what needs to be changed is the first step toward actually making those changes.

Area #7: Psychological and Emotional Life

Some of you need to spend more time by yourself. Others have negative, addictive behaviors that need to be broken. Maybe you need counseling to help you overcome some past hurts. Determine not to let negative emotions rule your life any longer—change!

Area #8: Fun and Adventure

You should have goals for this category as well. Jot down all your desires, regardless of how unrealistic they may seem at the moment. Have you always wanted to cruise the Caribbean, watch whales in Hawaii, learn to drive a racecar, or attend a Broadway play? Write it down! Identifying these desires is the first step toward making them a reality.

Once you have identified your specific desires in all these major areas and have written your goals, you are ready to take the next step toward preparing yourself for change. So if your journal entries are finished for the time being, read on!

Reasons Why We Change

The next step toward preparing for change is to list all the reasons why you desire to change. Usually people change for one of two reasons—to move away from pain or to move toward gain. God used these motivators when He created heaven and hell; hell is the pain, and heaven is the gain! We resist changing because we fear loss, but when the pain of staying the same becomes greater than the pain of change, we become willing to let go of the familiar and to embrace the new.

Reason #1: A Triggering Event

A middle-age man has a heart attack and realizes, "I'd better change how I eat. I'd better change the fact that I never exercise." A teenager turns to drugs, and the parents realize they must change their busy work schedules. It is unfortunate that most people wait until crisis situations before they are motivated to do something new.

In the Chinese language, the word *crisis* is made up of two symbols; the first symbol means danger, and the second means opportunity. Every time you experience a crisis, you can either let it destroy you or use it as an opportunity for personal growth. If you allow it, the fear you feel when facing a problem or challenge can propel you toward change. The real problem is that some people have never been scared to the point of desiring the changes they need!

Reason #2: Reaching Your Limit

People say, "That's it; I've had it!"

Even God gets to this point sometimes! He continually showed mercy on the people in Noah's day, but He finally told Noah, "Build an ark because I've had it! I've had it with sin. I've had it with wickedness. I *will* see change because I'm about to make it rain!"

Sometimes it is good to get to the place where you say, "I've had enough! I refuse to allow the world to squeeze me into its mold anymore! Things are going to change."

Reason #3: Poor Alternatives

This reason for change is very evident in abusive relationships. Many times women will put up with an abusive husband until severe physical harm occurs. Then they wake up and say, "I'd better get out of here, or I'm going to get killed." They realize that staying is life-threatening. Sometimes we put ourselves in dangerous health situations by constantly overeating or eating the wrong foods. After years of abusing our bodies physically, we must change or face the negative consequences of sickness or death.

One time a woman brought her adopted child who was covered with bruises to my church. I was just a young pastor and was pretty naïve. (This was before there was so much public awareness of abuse.) I thought there was something physically wrong with the child and wondered if a disease caused the discoloration. Then I received a call from people at social services. They told me that the mother had severely abused the baby almost to the point of death. Obviously, social services people removed the child from that home. The situation required immediate change because the alternative of having the baby continue to stay with that mother was absolutely unacceptable.

Reason #4: External Pressure

Job cutbacks, corporate downsizing, changes in the economy, and inflation are all examples of external pressure. The first chapter of Psalms talks about the pressure of the world around us and describes a man whose internal life is so strong that pressure does not crush him. He stays anchored in his confidence to do well, and he is able to make the necessary adjustments to his life to continue to thrive.

Some people get stuck where they are and seem to dry up. They do not bring forth their fruit in its season. They sit around complaining because things are not the way they used to be. They are not willing to change.

We need to raise our expectations of ourselves. We should be determined to make positive changes in our lives *before* we arrive at the point where change is the most difficult. If you need to make more money, for example, you need to start doing something about it now—not when the final notices start arriving. Things do not get better automatically. Money does not just drop out of the sky. Relationships do not get healthy all by themselves. You must take the necessary steps to make changes in your life. You must exercise your power of choice. If you do not choose to change, you may be forced to change by external pressures that come upon you.

The Holy Spirit is God's agent of change. He will help you see areas in your life that need improvement. He will also warn you of changes that are going to happen around you so that you can be prepared for them. You need to cultivate sensitivity to the voice of the Holy Spirit and to the voice of your conscience. If you listen

• •

and are proactive about making needed changes in your life, you can avoid being forced to change as a result of external pressure.

Developing a Strategy for Change

If you really want to change, you must develop a strategy. Proverbs 24 tells us that with a strategy you can build your dream house of positive change. Having a strategy is like having a road map. If you take a trip without a map, you can easily get off course. With a map, however, finding the way to where you want to go is easy.

The main reason people abort their progress toward change is that they face resistance. They begin to feel bad or uncomfortable during the process of change, and they just give up. If you take the time to develop a strategy, that strategy will become the map to help you maneuver past this resistance.

A well thought-out strategy works like a global positioning apparatus in space. This apparatus searches out a minimum of three satellites to determine its exact location. A good strategy will operate the same way in your life. It can tell you exactly where you are and what direction you must go to arrive at your desired destination. It will keep you out of denial and will keep you moving forward. When you identify the things you need to change and develop a specific action plan to change them, it is simple to stay on course.

Steps to Developing a Strategy

Step 1: Expose Yourself to a New Environment

The first step toward developing a strategy for change is to expose yourself to a new environment. One of the best ways to jump-start change is to interrupt your normal patterns. When God wanted to change our church, He put us through a nine-week prayer meeting we called "Pray Through." We came to church every night for sixty-three nights! That will interrupt anyone's pattern.

After the first three weeks, one of our staff members came dragging into my office and said, "Pastor, I don't know if I can make it any longer." Figuratively speaking, I had to get an oxygen tank to resurrect him from the dead! The bad part was that I felt the same way he did; I needed an oxygen tank too! But that incredibly focused time was just what we needed. It interrupted our normal, confining pattern and helped us move forward into new things.

If you need to change, you need a pattern interruption. You need exposure to something different. If you are confined to a hospital with an illness, go outside and get some fresh air. If possible, ride a bike or go fishing! Do anything that will break the influence of that illness on your life. If you see the same four walls and the same doctors every day, they will become the only world you know. You must get out of your current environment and find a new world.

Some of you have not been confined to a hospital bed, but your daily life has become just as monotonous. You get up, eat breakfast, drink coffee, go to work, come home, watch a little TV, and go to bed. You get up the next morning and do the same things all over again. In order for you to experience change, your daily rhythm needs to be interrupted. This does not require that you make a radical change; even something as simple as exercising for thirty minutes a day or reading something positive and inspirational every morning will make a tremendous difference.

Acts 9 gives us the story of a man who experienced a major life pattern interruption. Saul, a man who persecuted Christians, was moving along on his regular course of business when God showed up in the form of a bright light and knocked him off his horse. When Saul hit the dirt, the first word out of his mouth was "Lord." That was a major change in routine! He went from persecuting Christians to calling Jesus "Lord" in a matter of seconds, but Saul was so headstrong and so driven that God had to blind him for three days just to break his pattern.

Unfortunately, some people would rather quit than adapt to a new pattern. People end up abandoning their marriage partner, quitting their job, and leaving their church because a familiar

•••

pattern gets interrupted, and they do not know how to cope. They do not understand that being in a new environment is the real key to their change.

If you are having trouble with your marriage, you need to hang around couples who have solid, healthy relationships. Influences from that new environment will rub off on you. If you are dissatisfied with your job, you should hang out with people who are practicing fulfilling careers. Get around them and discover what they are thinking, seeing, and expecting. Fill your mind with new information. You must learn to see differently, hear differently, and even smell differently if you want to experience change. A new environment will help you do just that.

My wife recently did something that was absolutely phenomenal. She brought home a new food—celery root! At first I thought, "You expect me to eat that? It looks like horses' hooves!" But when she put it in a pot, boiled it, and whipped it, it looked like mashed potatoes. She served it to me with cream, butter, salt, and pepper, and I thought I was in heaven! I am telling you the truth; I had a spiritual experience right there eating celery root.

We all need more exposure and new experiences. We all need fresh ideas. My wife found a recipe for celery root while she was reading a book. She gained new knowledge. When we gain knowledge, we gain confidence. Sources for new knowledge are in the form of books, tapes, videos, and even stimulating conversations. We should all make good use of these sources to change our environment.

Step 2: Locate and Use Available Resources

The second step toward developing a strategy for change is to locate and use the resources that are available to you. When Nehemiah wanted to rebuild the walls of Jerusalem, he went to the greatest resource he had—the king (Nehemiah 2). With the king's help, Nehemiah was able to accomplish his desired task.

There are many resources available to help you change. Most people never take the time to locate and use these resources. Books and tapes will teach you how to improve any area of your

life. Even if everything is checked out at the library, you have
access to thousands and thousands of resources on the Internet!
There is no longer any excuse for ignorance!

Step 3: Find Someone Who Will Coach You

The third step toward developing a strategy for change is to
find someone who will coach you. This person will be your moral
support when the going gets tough. He or she can provide you with
the wisdom of experience and can give you advice.

If you cannot find someone who is willing to coach you in
person, all is not lost. Get books and tapes from people who have
made it through what you are going through and allow them to
become your electronic mentors! Finding people after whom you
can pattern your success is a shortcut to change. Why reinvent the
wheel? Find someone who has already invented it and borrow it!

Step 4: Get a Picture of the Pain!

The fourth step toward creating your strategy is to intensely imagine the pain you will experience from staying the same.
Picture it in detail—complete with sight, sound, and feeling. The
Bible tells us in 2 Corinthians 7:10 that "godly sorrow produces
repentance leading to salvation." The word *sorrow* means pain,
and the word *repentance* means to change your mind. So another
translation of that passage could say, "The pain that you allow God
to direct brings a changing of the mind."

Whenever you connect your current behavior to pain, you
become willing to let go of that behavior and to embrace change.
If you tell small children not to touch a hot stove, and they do it
anyway, you will never have to tell them again. They will see pain
as the consequence and will have no desire to repeat that behavior.

This concept of painful consequences is difficult for many
people to grasp. As a society, we have moved away from valuing
delayed gratification. We want what we want instantly, and we are
unwilling to go through any pain to obtain our desires. We must be
creative if we are going to imagine the painful consequences of not
changing. The thought of pain can be a catalyst to move us away

•••

from our self-destructive behaviors and patterns. Ask yourself the
following questions to help you imagine that pain:

- What short-term consequences will I suffer if I
  do not change?
- What long-term consequences will be the result
  of my staying the same?
- If I do not change, how will staying the same
  affect my family and friends?
- What creative ways can I use to make myself
  aware of these consequences?

A current crime prevention program exposes juvenile
offenders to hardened criminals who are serving time in prison.
The juveniles witness first hand the consequences they will face if
they do not change their behavior. All reports indicate that the program is very effective.

Do yourself a favor by intensely imagining the pain and suffering you will experience if you do not change. Allow the fear of
that pain to propel you toward your needed transformation!

Step Five: Get a Picture of the Gain!

The fifth step is the opposite of the fourth. Instead of picturing the pain you will suffer as a result of not changing, picture
the benefits you will experience if you do change. Imagine these
benefits in vivid detail—using sight, sound, and feelings. Most people do this automatically when they make the decision to change
from being single to being married. They intensely picture the inti-
macy and companionship they will experience in marriage.

When I was a teenager, I lost more than fifty pounds using
this technique. I bought a pair of expensive swimming trunks and
pictured myself standing on the diving board of the local swimming
pool in front of all the girls. I was tired of not having a girlfriend
because I was fat. I clearly saw myself with a new body, with all the
girls desiring me! This picture became so real to me that I lost the
weight in a little over two months.

••

Step Six: Determine How You Will Deal With Resistance

The next step you must take in developing your change strategy is determining how you will deal with emotional resistance. When you start down the road to change, you *will* encounter resistance. If you decide to go on a diet, images of cheesecake will faithfully begin appearing in your mind. Your emotions will violently resist the change! Many people give up because they have negative experiences like this.

Some people give in to this resistance, eat one piece of cheesecake, and then use it as a trigger to cause them to completely abandon their decision to eat properly. As you begin to live out your change, you will most likely experience some level of failure. Overcome your feelings of guilt by focusing on the things you have accomplished, not on the places you have fallen short. Refocus your attention on your picture of the benefits the change will bring.

Step Seven: Replace Harmful Thoughts and Behaviors with Beneficial Ones

A major key to assimilating a desired change into your life is replacing harmful thoughts and behaviors with those that are encouraging and beneficial. This is the substitution principle. You substitute something positive for something negative—something good for something bad.

One of the reasons dieting is so difficult is that you cannot stop eating completely! You can totally eliminate abusive substances such as alcohol or drugs and be better off for it, but you cannot totally eliminate food. Not being able to replace that familiar pattern of putting food in your mouth makes dieting a difficult change.

In my opinion, the best approach to losing weight is replacing the kinds of foods that make you fat with the kinds of food that help you lose and maintain weight. I enjoy eating meat, so I replaced eating foods loaded with carbohydrates with eating foods full of protein. I discovered that I could not drastically overeat protein-rich foods, and I began to lose my extra pounds. It has been fairly easy to maintain my weight by eating like this because I was able to substitute a familiar, damaging eating pattern for a beneficial one.

The same substitution principle applies to thoughts. If you struggle with a certain negative thought, replace it continually with a positive one until the new thought becomes a habit. This is where biblical confession can help. You can break negative thinking patterns by countering them with the Word of God. For example, every time you think, "I'm not going to make it," replace this thought with Philippians 4:13, which says, "I can do all things through Christ who strengthens me."

The best example I know of the power of substitution is a story about a man who had a terrible drinking problem. He decided he would replace drinking with painting. Whenever the desire for alcohol would surface, he would paint. Painting turned out to be a great outlet for his emotional needs. As he continued this pattern of substitution, it became so engrained in his life that he was able to totally overcome his addiction.

Step Eight: Decide How You Are Going to Reward Yourself

The last step you should take to prepare yourself for personal change is to decide how you will reward yourself for your accomplishment. Rewarding yourself for change is an important motivator. Before David went out to fight Goliath, David asked, "What is to be done for the man who kills this giant? What will he receive?" (1 Samuel 26) Even God Himself gives us rewards. Hebrews 11:6 says that He is a "rewarder" of those who seek Him.

It is also healthy to reward yourself. It is important to always keep moving toward something in your life. Knowing in advance how you will reward yourself enables you to overcome any short-term discomforts of change. You know your reward is waiting!

Rewards may be something you desire or something you need. A two-week trip to Hawaii is a great reward for losing fifty pounds, but so is the benefit of better health. Use something important to you as a motivator for personal change. Always think big when it comes to rewards!

Preparing for Personal Change

Summary

* Every change begins with an ending. With any change, you experience loss.

* Begin by specifically identifying what you want to change. You need to know what you desire. See your life as a book with blank pages and write the ending you want.

* Set goals for change in eight areas of your life: spiritual and ethical, family and home, finances and career, mind and education, body and health, society and relationships, psychology and emotions, and fun and adventure.

* List the reasons you desire to change. People usually desire to move away from pain or to move toward gain.

* People are usually motivated to change for several reasons: experiencing a triggering event, reaching their limit, seeing that an alternative is not good, or coming under some external pressure.

* You need to raise your expectations of yourself and cultivate sensitivity to the voice of your conscience or spirit. The greatest agent of change is the Holy Spirit.

* The first step to developing a strategy for change is to interrupt your normal daily patterns and expose yourself to a new environment.

- The second step to developing a strategy for change is to locate and use the resources that are available to you. You can find out anything you need to know.

- The third step to developing your change strategy is to find someone who will coach you. If you cannot find someone to do this, use the books and tapes of those whom you admire.

- The fourth step in your strategy should be to intensely picture in your mind (complete with sight, sound, and feeling) the pain that will remain if you stay the same.

- The fifth step is to intensely picture in your mind (complete with sight, sound, and feeling) the benefits the desired change will bring.

- The sixth step to determining your strategy for change is to determine how you will deal with resistance. Most people give up because they encounter negative feelings along the way to change. Decide in advance what action you will take to overcome this discomfort.

- The next step in your strategy is to replace harmful thoughts and behaviors with those that are encouraging and beneficial. Use this substitution principle to change your thinking.

- The last step in your strategy is to decide how you are going to reward yourself when you accomplish your change. Such a reward will help you overcome any short-term discomfort you may feel. Think big when it comes to rewards!

2

How to Release the Power to Interrupt

The strongest power in your life is the power of your will. If you do not like the direction your life is headed, you can *choose* to interrupt it. Just as God sat on the edge of a universe that was empty and void and chose to interrupt it with the creation of the sun, moon, planets, and stars, we can also choose to interrupt the nothingness in our lives. You can interrupt depression. You can interrupt inadequate feelings. You can interrupt financial and relational challenges. Releasing the power to interrupt is not hoping things will get better; it is making the choice to change them.

Many people feel stuck in their jobs, but you can make a decision to change jobs. You are never stuck! You can make a decision to do anything you want to do, even if it is wrong. You can even choose to go to hell, and God will honor your decision to do so. He respects your power of choice because that power is what makes you most like Him.

You Are Like God in Your Power to Choose

To release the power to interrupt, you must realize that you are like God in your power to choose. You can change anything in your life! You can be anything you want to be. People tend to fall into the river of life, flowing whichever way the current takes them. Forces of mediocrity, feelings of inadequacy, and false beliefs are always trying to persuade you that you cannot be any different than you are right now. But you can resist this conspiracy. You can swim upstream toward your own transformation. You can *choose* to change.

Regardless of where negative influences originate, they can be resisted. A thoughtless mom may continually tell her son that he will never amount to anything, but that child has a choice of whether or not to accept the Mom's negative assessment. Many people simply choose to believe disabling information. They use it as an excuse not to change. In Romans 12:2, the Bible tells us not to be conformed to this world, not to let the world squeeze us into its mold. You have the tremendous capacity to resist anything that hinders your potential. You can choose your dreams. You can will your destiny.

When I was a teenager, I owned two muscle cars. One of them had a manual transmission; it was necessary to engage the clutch in order to put the car into gear. I discovered just how important a clutch is to a car when I blew mine in a street race. My engine still had all of its power, but the car could not move!

Your will acts as the clutch in your life. You can be all revved up to change, but until you engage your will, you will never take action. If you submit your will to hindering beliefs, you will find that you are powerless to move! Making a quality decision to change, however, engages the clutch of your life and starts you down the road to personal transformation. Benjamin Disraeli said, "Nothing can resist the human will that will stake even its existence on its stated purpose."

Life is Waiting on You

Next, to release the power to interrupt, you must realize that life is waiting on you. Even God is waiting to see how you will respond! He is waiting to see what choices you will make. He is waiting to see what you will do.

Little children have no problem choosing what they want. They go into a toy store and say, "I want *that* toy!" As adults, we have been conditioned to go with the flow. We have learned not to be disruptive, to accept whatever life brings us. When we accept everything that comes our way, we get squeezed into a mold. We must learn to make personal choices about what we want.

Your choices have to be stronger than mere wishes, however. Some people would like to have a million dollars. Others
would like their marriages to be repaired. You do not get where
you want to go in life just because you would like to. You do not
receive what you need just because you need it. If you have not yet
noticed, life does not work this way. Things do not just happen
because you put them on your wish list. You experience personal
change because you make a committed decision to do so.

I taught my teenagers that if they made proper choices
ahead of time, they would not feel pressured when alternatives
came their way. They would have already chosen what they were
going to do. You have the responsibility of deciding what you will
accept or reject in life. One man said, "Trouble may come knock-
ing on your front door, but you don't have to invite it in for a tea
party."

Releasing the power to interrupt means committing ahead
of time that life is not going to push you around. This kind of decision says, "I am not going to bow to the pressure." It says,
"Whatever trouble comes, I'm not giving up!"

Daniel, Shadrach, Meschach, and Abednego had this kind
of commitment (Daniel 3). Even when faced with the prospect of
being thrown into the fiery furnace as a penalty for not worshipping
the king's idol, they replied that the king could do to them whatever he wanted to do, but they were not going to bow their knees!
That is the kind of decision God was talking about in
Deuteronomy 30 when He told us to choose life.

Let Go of the Past

You must let go of the past. Paul said, "One thing I do, forgetting those things which are behind and reaching forward to
those things which are ahead, I press toward the goal for the prize
of the upward call of God in Christ Jesus" (Philippians 3:13). You
cannot grab hold of new behaviors and habits if you are still cling-
ing to old ones. Take time to identify the negative behaviors in
your life. Write out the things that are harmful about them and the

•••

benefits you will receive from being free. Doing so will help you make the decision to say goodbye to those negative behaviors forever.

The word *decision* comes from two words in the Latin language; the first means from, and the second means to cut. So the word *decision* literally means to cut from. When you make a quality decision, you are cutting yourself off from the things that are harmful to you.

Remember how I had to have a funeral for rice and gravy? I had to bury rice and gravy because they were making me fat. Do you know what funerals do for you if they are done correctly? They give you the opportunity to say goodbye. When you look into the casket of someone you love, you know that person is not there. The funeral is not for him or her; it is for you—to bring closure to the situation. In the same way, you must have a funeral to say goodbye to those things that you love but that are not good for you.

With every funeral, you experience grief. When you decide to quit smoking and someone offers you a cigarette, you go through a grieving process when you refuse it. That grieving process is healthy. If you do not allow yourself to go through it, you are still living in a certain level of denial. You have not accepted the fact that you are changing. You have not really said goodbye.

To help yourself go through the grieving process successfully, identify all the things that were harmful in the situation. Some people feel only the loss; they forget how the situation was damaging them. Some people allow fear of the future to paralyze them. If they do not deal with this fear, it will lead them into depression, which will cause them to retreat back into their harmful behavior patterns. They will return to what is comfortable and familiar.

The correct course of action is, of course, to allow yourself to grieve but to stay on track through this grief by exploring the new possibilities for your life. Once you have located new and healthy behavior, make a commitment to carrying out those new actions.

Start Seeing the Possibilities

In addition to letting go of the past, you must start seeing the possibilities. Many people feel trapped. Most of them are waiting for something to happen outside them to bring change, and some people stay stuck for a long time. One man said, "Many people die at age twenty-one, but they are not buried until they are sixty-five!" People get stuck in certain behavior patterns because they believe it is impossible for them to break free.

Some people stay stuck due to hurts from their past. Maybe they were not loved as children. All of us would agree they had a right to be loved, but they will continue to live their entire lives as victims if they focus on the fact they were denied that right. Nothing will help them now but change.

At the pool of Bethesda, Jesus asked a lame man if he wanted to be made well (John 5). (Jesus was smart enough to know that some people do not want to be made well; being made well takes them out of what is comfortable and familiar.) The man replied that he had no one to put him into the pool when the healing waters stirred. He was so busy looking at the problem, he missed seeing the Healer right in front of him! (That would be like you complaining to a doctor that the medicine he or she prescribed was causing allergic reactions, while the doctor was trying to tell you that you were already well and could stop taking it!) This man finally awoke to the fact that Jesus might be able to do something for him even if he never got wet, and when his eyes were opened to that possibility, he was instantly healed.

Seeing the possibilities of change is vital if we want to continue making progress toward our goals. A national denominational magazine did a two-page, full-color article on our church. It mentioned that a certain man had given a large sum of money toward our building program. After the piece was printed, this man began to drop hints that there were things he did not like about our church. One day, without any notice, he took the money back!

I was devastated. I called one of the primary mentors in my life and told him what had happened. He said, "Billy, you can live the rest of your life hurt and disappointed, or you can see that there are other possibilities available to pay for your land and to build your new building." I began to explore those other possibilities, and the money quickly became available to complete the project.

Challenge the Lie of Being Trapped

When you begin to see the possibilities, you have to challenge the lie of being trapped. When you expose yourself to new possibilities, you can make new choices; you are not trapped.

A single mom complaining about her job came into my office. I hear people complain all the time, but this woman was unusually grieved. She complained about this person and that person, this situation and that situation. I could not believe her long list of complaints.

Finally, I looked at her and asked, "Why don't you quit?"

She said, "I can't quit. I've got to provide for my kids. I make good money there. I can't do anything else."

I asked, "Have you thought about another hospital? Have you thought about serving in another area of the medical field?"

Her response to every question was, "It won't work."

I remembered a contact I had in the medical profession and recommended that she talk to this person. Reluctantly, she agreed. From that one interview, she was offered three different positions, all of them paying more money than what she was currently making! She told me later that she wished she had talked to me sooner. I simply let her know there were other possibilities.

There is not one person reading this book who is permanently trapped. There is not one person reading this book who does not have possibilities. If you think you are trapped, you believe a lie. God can and will help you change your circumstances if you are willing to move out of your comfort zone. Are you willing to look at the possibilities rather than focusing on the problem? God is the God of change! You must be willing to let the Healer touch you and to stop complaining that you have no one to put you in the pool.

. . . .

Move Yourself Into Another Environment

After you have challenged the lie that you are trapped, you must move yourself into another environment. If you had been born in another country, you would be very different from the way you are today. You would possess the same cells and the same blood, but you would be drastically different. Why? Because you are, in part, a product of your environment; your environment has a tremendous influence on you.

Before you think I am telling you to move to another state, divorce your spouse, or quit your job, you need to understand that your environment is both inside and outside you. A move to another state might help, but the main change must take place in your thoughts and feelings. You must move your mind to a new environment. You can do this using books, tapes, sermons, movies, and even new friends who will talk to you about something different.

A wise, old man was walking along a trail when a young man met him and asked, "Oh, wise man, please tell me what kind of city I'm going to."

The old man looked at him and said, "Tell me what kind of city you came from." The young man explained his perceptions of the place he had lived. The old man answered, "That's the same kind of city you're going to."

You should move yourself into the kind of environment in which you can dream again. Move to the kind of environment that places you around new friends—people who will pull you up instead of push you down. Find people who are doing what you would like to do. Get around them and talk to them. Hang around people who are strong and healthy in their beliefs. Leave the company of people who do nothing but complain.

It is imperative that you move *toward* a new environment, not just *away* from an old one. Some people move away from something, only to move right back into the same kind of place. Amazingly, there they find the same problems! If you move into a new environment because you are running away from something,

•••

most assuredly you will take that something right with you.
Wherever you go will be the same.

Before Moses could deliver the nation of Israel, he had to
leave Egypt and go live in the land of Midian for forty years
(Exodus 2). The word *Midian* means strife. Whenever you start to
grow and change, you will experience strife between your old
beliefs and your new ones. Moses had some personal growth
issues. He had some changes to make.

God used the environment of Midian to prepare Moses for
what was to come. God placed him in this growth environment and
gave him Jethro, the priest of Midian, to be his mentor. During
those forty years, things were deposited in Moses' life that prepared him to become the leader of the nation of Israel. Even when
Moses was leading the children of Israel through the desert on the
way to the Promised Land, Jethro continued to speak into Moses'
life. He continued to mentor him and challenge him to change
(Exodus 18).

I once had a ski instructor who was trying to teach me a
new technique. I thought it was crazy! But after a while, I reasoned,
"He's the one skiing the most difficult terrain; I'm the one falling
down all the time!" I decided I had better let him mentor me in
this area. I tried what he said, and it worked.

In order to ski better, I had to change my approach. Most
people need to change their mental approach in order to see the
possibilities for their situation. Take inventory of your mental and
spiritual environment; your residency influences your entire out-
look on life!

Learn to Use the Law of the Mind

For change to occur, you must learn how to use the law of
the mind. When you make a decision to change, the law of the
mind goes to work to make your decision a reality. Read this next
statement carefully: Your thoughts plus your feelings equal your
beliefs. Your beliefs affect your behavior, and your behavior affects
the results you get in your life. If you do not like the results you are
getting, you must change your beliefs.

In order to change your beliefs, you must purposely direct the law of the mind. We tend to function at our lowest mental capacity by automatically taking the path of least resistance. Disabling influences are always trying to impede our progress. They try to make us victims to the pressures of life.

The power that can control your thoughts is your will. Due to your will, you can choose what to think. You are not programmed like a computer. A computer simply runs the software you put into it. A computer cannot tell you, "I will not run that program."

Life sends you thousands of negative messages every day. A single Sunday edition of a major newspaper contains more negative information than people in Jesus' day were exposed to in their entire lifetime. You must understand how to disable these negative messages.

Thoughts come into your mind as images. These images are vivid with sight, sound, and feeling. That is why you enjoy watching movies and television programs; they best represent how you think. As these thought pictures enter your mind, all your senses get involved. If you see an image of something scary, you will actually feel fear. Even though the picture is not real, the feeling is! The good news is that you are not at the mercy of such thoughts. You can interrupt them.

You begin to release the power to interrupt your life at the point of thought. When you choose the thoughts on which you will focus, you are initiating the law of your mind. Everything you produce in your life begins as a thought.

Thoughts come from four sources: information, personal experiences, memories, and imagination. By the power of your will, you can choose what information you will put into your mind. You can also choose what meaning you will derive from your personal experiences. It is not what happens to you that harms you; it is the definition or meaning you attach to these events.

Memories are those mental tapes from your past experiences you replay. The largest sum of these memories tends to be unfavorable. They hinder you by replaying all your past mistakes and inadequacies, but you have the power to change that pattern.

You can choose to dwell on memories that will empower rather than disable you.

Last, your thoughts come from your imagination. Your imagination is the only area in which you have the ability to originate a thought. You know from first-hand experience that you can give birth to both positive and negative thoughts in your imagination.

These four sources of thought are all written out on the tablet of your mind, but your will has the power to choose your reading material at any given moment! You can open or shut the gate of your thinking on any given thought. You can choose your point of focus. The power to interrupt begins by engaging your will to carefully pick the thoughts on which you will dwell.

There are two ways to bring about permanent change in your life. Using the law of the mind is the easiest way, but you can also go straight to your actual behavior and *will* it to change. The feelings of discomfort you will experience when you use this second method will be most distressing since you are forcing change *cold turkey*, but it is possible. If you want to lose weight, for example, you can go on a ten-day fast and *force* your behavior to comply. An easier and more effective method is to utilize the law of the mind by engaging your **will** to interrupt your **thoughts** through feeding yourself new information—information about all the benefits you will experience from losing weight. Then add your **feelings** to this new information by beginning to experience the sensations of what it would be like to have lost the weight. By doing this, you will develop a new empowering **belief** about weight and body size. In turn, you will change your **behavior** toward food, and the **result** you will receive is permanent weight loss.

Summary

You can change *anything* in your life when you realize you have the power of choice. Let go of the past and start seeing the possibilities. Challenge the lie that you are trapped and move yourself into an environment that will bring you new information. Be aware of the thoughts and feelings that are forming your beliefs;

then consciously choose new thoughts and actions that will move you toward the results you desire. The possibilities are endless when we learn how to release the power to interrupt. Go for it; life is waiting on you!

How to Release the Power to Interrupt

Summary

- To release the power to interrupt, you must first realize that you are like God in your power to choose. You can change *anything* in your life.

- Second, realize that life is waiting on you. Even God is waiting to see how you will respond.

- Third, you must let go of the past. Identify what is harmful and make a quality decision to let it die. Do not use emotional resistance as an excuse to call off the funeral!

- Fourth, you must start seeing the possibilities for the future. You are not a victim but a victor! You can make new choices.

- Next, you must challenge the lie of being trapped. God can and will help you change your life, but you must be willing to move out of your comfort zone.

- Fifth, move into another environment. You must move *toward* a new environment, not just *away* from where you are.

- Sixth, learn to use the law of the mind. Your thoughts plus your feelings equal your beliefs. Your beliefs, in turn, affect your behavior, and your behavior affects the results you get in life. If you do not like the results you are getting, you must change your beliefs.

3

Identifying Belief Strongholds

To renovate an old house, you need tools: saws, hammers, wrenches, drills, and a sledgehammer. You begin by tearing down a wall, tearing out a sink, or tearing up an old kitchen floor. You get rid of the old to make room for the new! You hang new sheet-rock, paint, put up wallpaper, and do whatever else is necessary to make it look pretty. With a few tools, new supplies, and much time and effort, you make the place look new and charming. Renovation is hard work, but if you desire change badly enough, you can do it.

Romans 12:2 says to be "transformed by the renewing of your mind." Renew means change; it also means to renovate. Renovation always begins with the tearing down of the old. As we renovate our minds, we tear down old, hindering beliefs and make room for new, productive beliefs.

God gives us the spiritual tools necessary for mind renovation. Second Corinthians 10:4 says, "For the weapons of our warfare are not carnal but mighty in God for pulling down strongholds." The phrase "pulling down" means demolition. What do we need to demolish? What do we have to renovate? What is it about our minds that needs to be changed? We need to change wrong beliefs that have formed strongholds in our thinking!

Strongholds of Hindering Beliefs

The meaning of the word stronghold is a castle or a fortress. There are castles and fortresses in your mind that need to be demolished or renovated. They are built out of hindering beliefs. Hindering beliefs are beliefs you have formed, perhaps over a period of years, that are wrong and disabling. They may be beliefs about God, about yourself, or about circumstances in your life. If you want to experience change, you must start by demolishing these strongholds of hindering beliefs, for they are what's stopping you from achieving your dreams and desires.

As stated before, your mind is made up of your thoughts, your feelings, and your beliefs. These three working together affect your behavior. Your behavior, in turn, affects the results you get in life. If you do not like the results that you are getting, you must change your behavior. But your behavior will not change until you change your beliefs; therefore, all permanent change begins in the mind.

Formula for Beliefs

Because changing your beliefs is directly connected to changing your behavior, it is important to understand how beliefs are formed. Here is a simple formula: **Your thoughts + your feelings = your beliefs.**

Your beliefs are formed as your emotions are stirred and as you become persuaded that certain thoughts are true. The Apostle Paul said that God stirred in the minds of his listeners their "most holy emotions thus persuading them." The closest most people have come to experiencing faith is fear. As I describe below actual experiences I had in believeing something that was not how I saw it, you will see that when I *feared* something I experienced the sensations of fear in sight, sound, and feeling. I possessed all of the sensations of that fear when, in fact, it was not true. Faith works in exactly the same way. It is experiencing in sight, sound, and feeling the things I am believing for before I get them. I have the spiritual and emotional sensations of experiencing what I need before I get it. That's faith.

Faith is a conviction of the truth about anything. Some of you have faith in the wrong things; you are convinced they are true when they are not! Right or wrong, your thoughts plus your feelings always equal your beliefs.

I was eating at a splendid restaurant in a foreign country when I realized I did not have my billfold. I thought I had lost it.

....

It contained several thousand dollars, my passport, and a diamond bezel that I had just purchased for my wife's watch. Even though I was at an expensive restaurant with a scrumptious meal in front of me, I suddenly felt sick and wanted to leave.

A friend suggested I call the hotel and ask that they send someone to my room to check for my wallet. I really did not think I left it there. The country I was visiting is notorious for pickpockets, and I distinctly remembered a man bumping into me on the ferry ride to the restaurant. I was *sure* he had taken my wallet. For twenty minutes, we waited for a call from the hotel. For twenty minutes, I fully believed that my billfold and all of its belongings were gone forever. For twenty minutes, I could not eat a bite! Then the call came. The hotel manager found my billfold in my room—right where I had left it.

Before that call, everything in me genuinely believed my wallet was gone. But that belief was wrong, thank God! The feelings I experienced in connection with that belief, however, were very real. I suffered through the sensations of actually losing my wallet when, in reality, it had never been out of my hotel room.

Hindering beliefs cause some people to experience what I did with my billfold. They believe wrong things about themselves, about their marriages, about their past, about their finances, or even about their God. And they experience the sensations of those wrong beliefs, just as I experienced the sensations of losing my billfold.

Have you ever been afraid of the boogie man behind the door? If you believe he is real, he can make goose bumps come up all over your arms! I have actually run out of the house (as an adult!) because I thought someone was in there.

I remember one time when I thought someone was in the basement. I heard something fall. When it did, I got goose bumps from the top of my head to the bottom of my feet. I ran to my wife. She took one look at my face and asked, "Honey, what's the matter?"

I said, "There's someone down there! There's someone in our basement! Go check it out. Go!"

....

My brave wife searched the basement. She came back and said, "Honey, there's no one down there."

I said, "Yes, there is; I heard him."

She said, "No, there's not." She had to take me by the hand, lead me down the stairs, and walk me through the basement before I was convinced.

I believed there was someone in the basement. My belief was wrong, but I believed it so strongly that I experienced all the same sensations I would have if someone were actually down there. When I talk about strongholds, I am referring to wrong or hindering beliefs. They are not true, but you think they are. And because you are convinced, you experience all the same sensations in your life that you would experience if those hindering beliefs were actually true.

Let us pretend that you were abused by an authority figure when you were a child. From that abuse you formed the false, hindering belief that there are no loving or caring authority figures. In your life today, you have problems relating to your boss at work; you have problems relating to your pastor; you have problems relating to police officers and to the Internal Revenue Service. As a matter of fact, you have difficulty relating to anyone who even remotely tries to tell you what to do! You have a hindering belief; a stronghold has developed in your mind.

The sad part is that many of us are not even aware of our hindering beliefs. Because we are not aware of them, we continue to live as though they are true when, in actuality, they are just the lost billfold and the boogie man in the basement! We do things a certain way, give certain responses, and continue to function in life at a level much lower than our potential because of these hindering beliefs.

Biblical Unbelief

Hindering beliefs and unbelief are really the same thing. When you mention unbelief, however, most Christians think they know what you are talking about. They say, "I don't have any unbelief; I'm full of faith." Maybe so, but do they have faith in the right

• •

things? When they think of the word *unbelief,* they probably think of not believing anything, but unbelief can also mean believing the wrong things. This gives us a new perspective on biblical unbelief. For every area of your life in which you hold a hindering belief, you are in unbelief. You cannot fully embrace the promises of God if you hold on to hindering beliefs. Having faith in a hindering belief is unbelief!

Many of us play the role of a victim because of our hindering beliefs. We think, "This is just the way I am." Or we say, "I'm this way due to how my parents raised me." The Word of God will slam into such strongholds of thinking, but the Word does us no good unless we believe it! Hebrews tells us that the Word has to be mixed with faith in order for it to profit us. "For indeed the gospel was preached to us as well as to them; but the word which they heard did not profit them, not being mixed with faith in those who heard it" (Hebrews 4:2). No matter how often we read the Bible, memorize its passages, or quote its verses, it will do us no good unless we mix it with faith. This is why Jesus warns, "take heed *how* you hear" (Luke 8:18 [emphasis added]).

Some people allow hindering beliefs to dominate their life. Their thoughts plus their feelings equal their beliefs, and unless those beliefs are renovated, truth cannot penetrate their thinking. As these strongholds are pulled down, however, the truth can enter, new beliefs can be formed, and people can be set free.

Demolition of Cancer

I experienced this process firsthand with one of the elders in our church. He was thirty-nine and good-looking, with a beautiful wife and three beautiful daughters. The doctors diagnosed him with aggressive lymphoma and told him that he had only a few months to live. The cancer was literally eating his body.

As his pastor and as his friend, I was devastated. He was one of the closest men to me in my entire congregation. He helped me through some personal challenges of my own. The question I wanted to cry out was "Why?" But *why* is one of the most disabling questions you can ever ask. *Why* does not change anything.

• •

Looking at my friend after a depressing doctor's visit, I realized I had to help him, and I had to help him quickly. He did not have three years to grow and change; he did not have three months! Change had to happen, and it had to happen fast. One of the most hindering beliefs you can have is that change takes a long time. The world tells us it is a slow process, but it does not have to be. You can change in an instant.

Talking with my friend about his condition, I discovered there were some strongholds in his mind that needed to be torn down. Thoughts of death were nearly consuming him. They were building a castle in his mind that needed to be demolished if he was going to overcome this disease.

I had to teach my friend how to interrupt those thoughts of death and pull down the wrong beliefs that were being formed. We did this by aggressively building new images of life that were based on the promises found in God's Word. I also taught him about the power of presenting his body, a subject I will cover in a later chapter. I taught him every biblical technique I knew to bring forth change.

My friend told me that when he was alone at night, he had to fight off images of his casket. He would lie down to go to sleep and would see pictures of himself lying in his casket instead of on his bed. Demolishing that stronghold took some major work on his part.

Norman Cousins, author of *The Anatomy of an Illness,* said, "Drugs are not always necessary, but belief in recovery always is." The importance of pulling down strongholds of wrong beliefs cannot be underestimated. Hindering beliefs are like caustic fumes that you cannot see or smell, but they will choke the life out of you if you let them. You must deal with them quickly and effectively.

Demolition of Depression

I went through a very trying personal experience several years ago in which I had to demolish some hindering beliefs that were causing me to be severely depressed. It was an awful time, and it felt like it was never going to end. It all started when some people dealt dishonestly with me, causing me to lose several hundred thousand dollars. You might say, "That was a good reason to be depressed." I thought so too, but that depression almost killed me.

During this time, I had a close friend who stayed with me for nine weeks. He tried to encourage me, but I was in such a place of despair that I resisted all his efforts to help. There is only one letter difference in the spelling of the words *bitter* and *better*. I was so bitter about my problem that I could not see any way to get better.

My friend wanted to help me change my emotional and spiritual environment by praying with me, but I was in no mood for prayer. I was looking for an easy way out of my dilemma, but there were some personal adjustments I needed to make. He gently but firmly told me I had to change my mental focus. He insisted, in fact, that I should start praying for those who had wronged me so severely.

I know I do not have to tell you that was not easy. But as I started to follow his suggestion (obviously a biblical one!), the grip of depression started to loosen. As I changed my mental focus and my behavior, I began to get free.

Then my friend told me something that really changed my focus. He told me that all the money that had been taken from me was going to come back to me! You know *that* got my attention, but I had a very difficult time believing him. Within minutes of the time he said it, a man knocked on my office door and handed me what I thought was an appreciation card. As I opened it, I saw the word *fifty* and immediately thought someone was blessing me with a fifty-dollar gift. When I looked at it more closely, however, the zeroes kept going. It was a check for fifty thousand dollars! Now my hindering beliefs were being challenged in a big way! Within one month, I saw a total of $130,000 returned, and all the legal issues I had been fighting for three years were resolved. Things were set in motion for all of the money I had lost to be recovered, and my disabling beliefs were totally blown right out of my mind.

Examples of Hindering Beliefs

You may have hindering beliefs that keep you from recovering things that have been stolen from you in life, just as my hindering beliefs kept me from receiving the justice I was due in my situation. In order to demolish these strongholds, you must first identify your wrong beliefs. Here are some examples of hindering beliefs people hold about God:

- God does not really want me to succeed.
- God really does not love me.
- God only wants bad things for me.
- God is a mean God.
- God is no fun.
- God cannot be known or understood.
- God does not really want me blessed.

Some people have hindering beliefs about themselves:

- I'm not good enough.
- I do not feel good about myself.
- I am not worthy.
- I am not a lovable person.
- I do not deserve to have the best.
- I could never do that.
- I do not have much to give.
- I am not important.
- I am a failure.
- I am a bad parent.
- I cannot accept myself.

You can also have hindering beliefs about other people:

- Other people are better than me.
- Other professions are better than mine.
- Other family members are better than me.
- My neighbors are better than me.

You may have hindering beliefs about your circumstances. Many people believe they are victims of their circumstances. Are you one of them? They say things like this:

- I can't do this because I'm not talented enough.
- I can't work for God because I'm not good enough.

- I can't speak because I'm shy.
- I can't step out in faith because I'm afraid.
- I can't meet the requirements of that job because I'm lazy.
- I can't understand because I'm not intelligent enough.
- I can't help people because I'm not friendly enough.
- I can't speak up for Jesus because I'm not bold enough.
- I can't succeed in business because I'm not smart enough.

People with a *victim mentality* say things about their past:

- I can't because I was never loved.
- I can't because my parents mistreated and abused me.
- I can't due to my past.

You do not *have* to be a victim; you can become a *victor* by demolishing your strongholds of hindering beliefs. You can learn to win. Do not allow past experiences to become the primary building blocks for your current beliefs. If you do, you will continue to live your present life out of what happened to you in the past. Here are more victim sayings:

- I'm a victim of life.
- I can't be happy because life is full of sorrow.
- I can't enjoy what I have because there's not enough to go around.
- I can't hope for change because it's impossible to change my world.
- I can't forgive myself because God won't forgive me.
- I can't love again because life is so disappointing.
- I can't expect anything good because the world is full of evil.

I am taking the time to give you many examples of hindering beliefs so you can begin to see that they appear in a myriad of ways. If you want to change your life by changing your mind, your

•••

first task is to identify the beliefs that have kept you bound to your current condition. You may believe that you get sick easily or that all people are mean. There are women who believe all men are pigs, and there are men who believe all women are nags.

Remember that your thoughts plus your feelings equal your beliefs. Your beliefs affect your behavior. Your behavior determines the results you get in life. Every negative behavior you have is directly connected to a hindering belief. The first step toward changing your behavior and getting better results is to change your hindering beliefs. In order to change them, you must first identify them.

You may already know what these beliefs are. Some of the statements on the previous pages may have rung a bell of recognition. If you have already identified them, you have made your first step toward change. Just in case you have not been able to identify them, however, let me remind you of a few ways to uncover them.

Emotional Resistance

Hindering beliefs show up as emotional resistance. You know you are facing emotional resistance when images and thoughts that directly contradict the changes you want appear in your mind. You begin a new diet, and vivid images of lemon pie or cheesecake keep coming into your mind. Like a magnet, hindering beliefs will pull you back to what is comfortable and familiar.

Many people think emotional resistance is a legitimate excuse for not changing. That is not true. They falsely think that if they were supposed to change, they would feel better about it. That is also a deception. Remember when I thought I had lost my wallet? I experienced all the emotional impact even though the thought was not true.

The initial resistance you feel toward change is driven by your negative emotions, which are directly connected to wrong beliefs. As you take action to change, your emotions and your hindering beliefs act as a magnetic compass. If the direction you are headed is contrary to your internal compass, the feelings of discomfort can overwhelm you. But as you build new, empowering beliefs in your life, your positive emotions will help you, and you will begin to experience the changes that you desire.

I have a blue chair that is my favorite snack chair in my house. I like to eat in it. If someone took my food and my blue chair, I would experience major emotional resistance. Something on the inside of me would scream, "I'm not supposed to change." Those negative emotions should serve as an indicator that there is a disabling belief in my life.

Most people allow negative emotions to captivate them. In fact, some people are so personally connected to their hindering beliefs that they see these emotions as their identity. Instead of just experiencing depression, they have great difficulty seeing themselves apart from it in any way. They become one with their hindering belief.

Remember my friend who challenged me to pray for those who had taken money from me? In order to get me to pray for them, he practically carried me into their business place! I had such strong feelings of hostility toward these people that it would be a vast understatement to say I felt emotional resistance. The only prayer I wanted to make for them was a prayer for God to take them out of this world! As I willfully began to focus on blessing them, however, something unusual began to happen. My focus changed, my beliefs about them changed, and the anger and disappointment I was experiencing began to leave. I persevered through the emotional resistance and actually underwent a significant transformation in my attitude toward them.

Do not mistake emotional resistance for a divine voice. If Jesus had made that mistake in the Garden of Gethsemane, He would never have made it to the cross. He suffered such great emotional resistance that the Bible tells us He sweated great drops of blood (Luke 22). At that moment of great stress, He could have easily mistaken the voice of His emotions for the voice of the Holy Spirit. But He knew the truth, and "for the joy that was set before Him endured the cross, despising the shame, and has sat down at the right hand of the throne of God" (Hebrews 12:2). Jesus encountered major emotional resistance, yet he overcame it. You can overcome too if you will use your negative emotions as indicators, not as captivators.

Hindering Beliefs Show Up as the Labels You Wear

Hindering beliefs are caught, not just taught. Some people catch hindering beliefs about themselves when they are young children. A parent or another authority figure calls them dumb, ugly, or clumsy, and they wear that label all their lives. After they are well into adulthood, they still wear a label that someone else gave to them. I encourage you to tear off your disabling labels! Do not allow yourself to be labeled by someone else. Choose the labels you desire to wear and wear them confidently.

Hindering Beliefs Manifest Themselves as Life Filters

Hindering beliefs manifest themselves as the filters through which you see life. It is not what happens to you that defeats you but the meaning you attach to it. The rain and sun come to everyone. It is your response to the weather that makes the difference. If you have a cloudy lens, it makes no difference how bright the day is. You will not see it as bright.

Hindering Beliefs Act as Obstacles to Receiving New Information

Hindering beliefs also act as your obstacles to receiving new information that can build your confidence and change your life. You can hear life-changing information, but it will do you no good if you do not believe it. The Bible tells us that Christians have a new identity and that they are God's workmanship (Ephesians 2:10). If you still choose to believe that you are worthless and inferior, however, that information will not affect you. Continuing to hold onto that hindering belief of inferiority will be a major obstacle to receiving new truth.

The Bible tells of the difficulty the people of Israel had in possessing their dream of an affluent, comfortable land. They are an example for us not to follow. Hebrews tells us they were considered rebellious because they had an "evil heart of unbelief"

(Hebrews 3:12-19). Your heart is made up of your thoughts and your feelings. Evil thoughts are your hindering beliefs—your unbelief! Unbelief hardens your heart, and a hard heart becomes a rebellious one.

The children of Israel could not enter the Promised Land due to wrong, hindering beliefs! If we allow negative beliefs to dominate our lives, we are stopped dead in our tracks and cannot change. We will never enter our land—our purpose and destiny. We will die in the wilderness.

When the Word is preached, our hindering beliefs act as a wall against which it slams. It will not profit us because we have no faith to mix with it. We have a heart full of hindering beliefs! We need to identify those hindering beliefs and change them so that the Word can penetrate and take full effect.

Let me remind you that every change begins with an ending. It is impossible to embrace something new if you are still holding the old. If I am hugging one person, I must let that person go before I can hug another. Letting go of the old involves loss, and all loss involves grieving. Grieving, if done properly, will bring you to a new place of healing. When we become aware of the hindering beliefs in our lives and let them go, we are free to embrace new, beneficial beliefs that will empower us for positive, permanent change.

Identifying Belief Strongholds

Summary

*   Romans 12:2 says you can change your life by changing your mind.

*   Strongholds are wrong, hindering beliefs in your mind that keep you from changing whatever you desire to change.

*   Your mind is made up of your thoughts, your feelings, and your beliefs. Your beliefs affect your behavior. Your behavior affects the results you are getting in life. If you want to change your results, you must first change your beliefs.

*   You must renovate your mind by tearing down wrong, hindering beliefs and putting new, correct beliefs in their place. In order to tear down the wrong beliefs, you must first identify them. Every negative behavior you have points directly back to a hindering belief.

*   The first way you can identify hindering beliefs is by your emotional resistance. You try to move forward and change, but it just does not *feel* right. Many people mistake this feeling for the Holy Spirit's telling them not to change, but it is really just their hindering beliefs' trying to pull them back into what is comfortable and familiar.

*   The second way hindering beliefs show up is through the labels you have been wearing. Wrong beliefs are caught,

not taught! You must tear off the labels other people have
tried to make you wear and choose the labels that you
desire.

- Third, hindering beliefs manifest themselves as the filters
  through which you view life. They are the lenses through
  which you positively or negatively evaluate everything that
  happens to you.

- Last, hindering beliefs act as obstacles to your receiving
  new information that can build your confidence and
  change your life. New, positive information is no good
  unless you believe it!

- People can have hindering beliefs about God, about
  themselves, about other people, or about life in general.
  Remember that your thoughts plus your feelings equal
  your beliefs. You can change your beliefs by changing
  your thoughts, and you can control your thoughts by
  choosing what you will focus on mentally.

- You must become aware of the disabling beliefs in your
  life in order to let them go and in order to embrace the
  empowering beliefs that will enable you to experience
  change.

4

Overcoming the Influences of the Past

After you identify your hindering beliefs, you need to identify where they originate. My son, Brant, learned to drive in Denver, and for a long time he did not drive on two-lane highways. My wife and I were driving through Arkansas, and Brant was following us. We had radios so we could communicate. There was a car between us, and I wanted him to pass. I said, "Son, I'm around the curve. It's a straight shot for a long way. Nothing is coming, so come on around."

He said, "Dad, what do I do?"

I said, "You just step on the accelerator and go around."

I could not believe that he was having difficulty passing another car. I gave him some specifics by adding, "Shift down to fourth gear, put it to the floor, and go!" I looked back in the mirror several minutes later, and he still had not moved. No other cars had come along for five minutes!

I asked my wife to get on the radio. She asked, "Brant, why haven't you passed?" No response.

I said, "Give me that radio!" I told him, "Son, get your rear end around here *now!*" I looked in my rearview mirror and saw his car jump. He quickly passed the other car. I had finally gotten him to do something he had never done.

Many people are hesitant to change because they are still living by what they know from the past. Before that moment, my son had no experience in passing a car. His past was hindering him.

A man was weaving all over the road until a highway patrolman stopped him. The highway patrolman asked, "Sir, did you know you were weaving all over the road?"

The man said, "Yeah, I think I was."

The officer asked, "Well, sir, are you drunk?"

The man said no.

He asked, "Are you high on drugs?"

The man said no.

The patrolman wondered, "What in the world is wrong with this guy? Why is he driving like this?" Finally, the patrolman stuck his head inside the man's car and saw twelve rearview mirrors! The patrolman asked, "What are you doing with twelve rearview mirrors?

The man responded, "I'm trying to drive by where I've been."

Like this man, many people are living their present and their future out of their past. They are trying to drive by where they have been. Many of your hindering beliefs originated in your past.

Your past, however, does not have to rob you. You may say, "That's easy for you to say. You don't know where I've been or what I've done." I really do not care, and neither does God! All *God* is concerned about is right now.

Attaching Meaning to Life Events

As I said before, every time an event happens to us in life, we split it open and give it meaning. Proverbs 23:7 says, "As a man thinketh in his heart so is he." The word *thinketh* means to split open. Every time something happens to you, you raise a mental machete, split that event open, and attach meaning to it.

If you are driving with twelve rearview mirrors, trying to drive by where you have been, you will split that event open and attach meaning to it based on all your past experiences. If you have been treated badly by someone, you may develop a hindering belief that everyone will treat you that way, and you may respond to people accordingly. The belief may become so strong that you believe innocent people intend to treat you badly. You must identify where your belief strongholds originated in order to clean out the filing cabinets of your mind. When you dump those negative files, you will no longer draw upon those memories to bring meaning into your current situations.

Drawing on Positive Memories

Before David went out to fight Goliath, David said to King Saul, "Your servant has killed both lion and bear; and this uncircumcised Philistine will be like one of them, seeing he has defied the armies of the living God" (1 Samuel 17). When David went back to the filing cabinet of his past, he pulled out memories that would enable rather than disable him. He pulled out files that would help to reinforce his faith in his current situation. He did not even have a sword in his hand at the time, but he had past references of his faith; he believed he could do it.

David looked through his file for an experience that said, "You can!" Because of their hindering beliefs, most people open files that say, "You can't." You can read in Philippians 4:13, "I can do all things through Christ who strengthens me," but your hindering belief stronghold will not allow you to really believe it. We know that Hebrews 4:2 teaches us that the Word has to be mixed with faith in order for it to take effect.

All beliefs in our mind, negative or positive, are supported by past experiences in our lives. I can ask you to think of some positive memories in your life, and you will find things that cause you to feel encouraged, enabled, and empowered. That is what David did. He looked to his past experiences with the bear and the lion and remembered how he had overcome them. Then he applied this memory to his current situation with Goliath.

Many people do not open the support files of good memories and experiences, but they choose to read only the bad ones. This is how people end up living their present out of their past. They may have experienced physical, verbal, or sexual abuse. They may have been wounded in a relationship. Memories from these two areas—past experiences and past relationships—can be replayed over and over again on the VCR of their mind. When they continue to watch the reruns, they distort how they interpret things in the present.

Some of the best advice I can give you is to get around somebody who will cause you to see life positively. Do not get your advice from the bartender; he will not encourage you. Talk to someone who can help you. If you are sick, talk to someone who has overcome your sickness and is well. If you are having trouble in your marriage, go to dinner with a couple who has a healthy relationship. Give yourself some new, positive experiences. Give yourself some new files to read!

Job said, "Even when I remember I am terrified, and trembling takes hold of my flesh" (Job 21:6). Job was obviously pulling up past files filled with negative experiences! Paul, on the other hand, said, "Forgetting those things which are behind and reaching forward to those things which are ahead, I press toward the goal for the prize of the upward call of God in Christ Jesus" (Philippians 3:13). Paul chose to forget the painful experiences that disabled him. He chose to dump those negative files.

Watch Your Associations

To be fully empowered in our lives, we must be free from the control of past negative experiences. We must be free from the influence of past hindering relationships. Your associations—the people whom you hang around—make a tremendous difference in your personal growth. You can put good teenagers with bad friends, and within two weeks the good teens can change dramatically for the worse.

The eleven-year-old who helped pull the trigger and killed some of his classmates in Jonesboro, Arkansas, did so because of the influence of his thirteen-year-old friend. The friend broke up with his girlfriend, sought to get revenge by shooting his classmates, and influenced the eleven-year-old to help him! The power of associations should never be taken lightly. Negative associations can pull you right down with them. When I was teaching my children how to choose their associations, I told them, "If you sit on the ice and start to freeze, you had better get off quickly, but if you sit on the ice and melt it, you can stay friends."

I have a negative memory of my sixth-grade teacher's criticizing the way I did a certain activity. I never again tried that activity because of what he said. He is dead and gone, and I am still listening to what he said! That is a hindering belief. I also remember a kid who made fun of me when I was about ten-years-old. He did this over thirty years ago, but I still remember and believe his words!

Opening Different Mental Files

God had to deal with another hindering belief I held concerning the growth of my church. I would confess that I believed our church was growing, but in my heart, I saw pictures of the opposite. I kept hearing disabling, hindering questions in my mind that asked, "Why are you here? What are you doing? What are you accomplishing? Are you doing anything to make a difference?" Those questions were tormenting me! They were impeding my leadership skills and keeping me unclear about my purpose.

My wife recommended that I open some different files in my mind. She encouraged me to find memories of past experiences at the church that encouraged me. She reminded me that only I could identify what those files were. I decided I would practice what I preached, and I followed her advice. I began to identify my successes and to focus on my accomplishments. In just a short time, my whole attitude changed, and those troubling questions went away. I could see where my church was making progress and began to set new goals for our congregation.

It All Depends on the Meaning

Whether an experience becomes an enabling or disabling memory depends on the meaning you attach to it. One day a woman who had a beautiful rose garden was working out in her yard. She went inside to get a glass of water and to straighten up some things in the house. When she came back outside, half of the beautiful roses she had been carefully cultivating were cut off.

Immediately, she knew who did it. It was the little boy next door who was always playing in her yard.

The woman ran and knocked on his door. The little boy answered, and she began scolding him for cutting off her roses. His mother came to the door and made the little boy apologize. Satisfied that the mother would discipline him accordingly, the woman went back home.

About an hour later, the woman's boyfriend, carrying a beautiful bouquet of roses, knocked on her door. Suddenly, she realized it was *he* who had cut her roses! He had taken them home and added greenery and baby's breath to make her a bouquet. This time, instead of reacting in anger to the fact her roses had been cut, she responded with joy. She profusely thanked her boyfriend for being so sweet and quickly made a mental note to apologize to the little boy next door!

In both instances, the same event happened, but what the woman believed about her cut roses made the difference in her response. It is never what happens *to* you; it is what happens *in* you that counts. How we respond has everything to do with the beliefs that we hold. Without exception, one hundred percent of the time we respond to life events out of our beliefs.

Sadly, we often do not know what we believe. Faith is a conviction of truth about anything. You can have faith in the wrong things and in your wrong beliefs. For instance, you may believe that you are a victim due to what happened to you in the past. Obviously, you should not deny what happened, but you can choose to become a victor. You empower or disable yourself depending on what you believe about what happened.

Your Beliefs Act as a Filter

To overcome the past, you must first realize that your beliefs act as a filter for your life experiences. Two people can go through exactly the same circumstances yet respond differently because of their beliefs. They see things differently on the inside. Your beliefs will determine how you judge the events of your life.

Paul brought this message across in one of his letters to the church at Corinth (2 Corinthians 4). People were trying to kill Paul. If people were trying to kill you, you would probably say, "Oh, they're after me; they're after me!"

Let me paraphrase for you how Paul responded to their threats. He said, "Bring it on. The more you bring, the more life will flow in me. You've got more stuff? I've got more life!" Paul filtered everything that happened to him through faith.

Paul had many problems. He did not say he was not pressed; he said the pressing was not going to crush him. Most people get pressed and say, "It's over."

Paul said that he was pressed but not crushed. Paul set an example for us; he flowed in the spirit of faith. One translation mentions the "mindset" of faith; another says the "attitude" of faith. What is this spirit, mindset, or attitude of faith that Paul had? What did he believe that caused him to overcome all his negative experiences and to not become disabled by them?

Paul saw a picture in his mind of the life of God flowing through him. He saw a picture of God putting him over in every situation. That is what enabled him to say that although all those things were happening to him, he did not pay attention to them, refused to focus on them, refused to look at them. He did not allow them to be the driving force of his life.

When your problems loom over you, they seem so big. Paul's problems must have seemed big to him too, but he chose not to look at them. He did not deny them, but he chose not to make them the focal point of his life. Paul filtered everything that happened to him through his pictures of faith.

Most people do not change until they have to change. If they do not have to change, they just coast and talk about how bad things are. For *things* to change, however, *you* must change. You determine how you will see things. Will you see them in a disabling way or in an empowering way? Will you use the circumstances of your life as stepping stones, or will they be stumbling blocks to your progress? Faith chooses to look at things positively.

....

You Must Determine How You Will Repsond

You must determine how you will respond. Romans 12:2 tells us not to allow the world to squeeze us into its mold. Let me give you a picture of what this is like. Think about being in the middle of the ocean with all the water around you, pressing against you. You dive down deeper and deeper until the pressure is so intense that you feel like you are going to explode. *That* is a good description of the world trying to squeeze you into its mold!

The pressure of the world tells you that you are not worthy and that you are not going to make it. It tells you that you will never amount to anything. Some people explode under that pressure. They have nervous breakdowns, and some even commit suicide. The substance that gives us the power to overcome the world's pressure is our faith. Paul said that the victory that overcomes the world is a result of our faith. "For whatever is born of God overcomes the world. And this is the victory that has overcome the world—even our faith" (1 John 5:4).

The original words for *victory* and *overcome* are the same, so you could quote the verse like this, "This is the victory that victories." Or you could say, "This is the overcomer that overcomes." In the original language, the word is *nike,* which means to continue in success. (The Nike company got its name from that word, and it is definitely continuing in success! One guy started the company by making tennis shoes, and later Michael Jordan was paid thirty million a year just to wear them and jump!)

Your faith is a weapon of victory. It is supernatural. It comes from God. When the pressure of the world starts to squeeze you, your faith comes to the rescue. It makes you like Superman coming out of the phone booth! With your faith, you are dressed in different clothes.

You must have a conviction on the inside of you that the Word of God is true. It is the only thing that always works. When a banker says you are going bankrupt or when the doctor says you do not have long to live, you get serious about what works. At that point, you are not too worried about someone's theology. For the pressures of life, you need something that works.

How are you going to help someone get out of the destructive lifestyle of drugs? How are you going to help a friend overcome that deadly disease? How are you going to help that couple save their troubled marriage? You must teach them to use supernatural weapons. You must teach them to use their faith.

Your Enabling Beliefs Are Your Protection and Your Power

You must begin to see your enabling belief as your protection and your power. You are either empowered or disabled by what you believe. Ephesians 6:16 says to take up the "shield of faith" in order to "quench all the fiery darts of the wicked one." Your enabling beliefs of faith are a shield against the devil's darts of unbelief.

The Dart of Thoughts

The devil throws different kinds of darts at you. The first kind is thoughts. The devil is not omniscient; he does not know what you are thinking, but he can put thoughts in your mind. He puts tempting thoughts in front of you like fishermen put worms in front of fish. Will you bite? Satan can try to alter your thinking. He knows that if he can get his thoughts in your *believer*, he has won the battle.

Sometimes you let those fiery darts into your mind. You think, "I'm not going to make it. I'm just a big dummy. I just mess up all the time." That is how the devil talks to you; he makes you think you are doing the talking! You must put up your shield of faith. If you have the right belief system, those darts will just fall to the ground. The only real power the devil has over you is the power of deception; he tries to get you to believe his lies. That is why the battle takes place in your mind; it is the only place that he can take advantage of you. That is why, when he sends his fiery darts in the form of disabling and hindering messages, you must raise your shield of faith.

The shield used during Bible days was a large, four-cornered rectangle that looked something like a modern door. The word Paul used for shield was the word for a large stone. Stones were used to shut or open the mouths of caves. Your faith is the stone that allows certain thoughts to come into the cave of your mind and keeps other thoughts out.

If a man were standing at your door with a gun, you would not let him in, would you? Many of us let thoughts into our minds that are just as potentially harmful. We can learn to quench the fiery darts of the negative thoughts the devil throws our way.

The Dart of Negative Circumstances

The second dart the devil will throw at you is negative circumstances. He cannot defeat you with those circumstances, but he can create them. He can build a fire that gets you distracted! When circumstances like terminal illness, bankruptcy, or past hurts surface, you can choose how you will respond. You can respond in fear, or you can respond in faith.

Fear is the opposite of faith. We can meditate on fear until everything seems hopeless. We think nobody else has ever made it through or can possibly understand. Faith gives you a new perspective. It builds a new belief system inside of you that is based on truth—the truth of the Word of God.

Let me tell you the difference between faith and positive thinking. If you are not careful, positive thinking can cause you to deny what you are going through. The Bible never tells us to deny what we are going through. It tells us to look right in the face of our circumstances and confront them with our faith. When Daniel was in the lions' den, he saw those big, ugly lions. He saw them licking their chops at him. He did not say that life was rosy or that he did not see any lions. He saw the lions, but he used his faith to defeat them.

Choose Your Residency

You have a choice of two houses in which you can live. One house is made of stone; the other is made of straw. The stone house represents a belief system founded on God's Word. The straw house represents a belief system founded on wrong, hindering beliefs.

Most people camp out in the straw house. Even if they start to make the move to the stone house, they hit emotional resistance and run right back home. They say, "No, that's not really me. It just doesn't feel like me. I know what the Word says, but I couldn't possibly be the righteousness of God in Christ. I'm not that worthy. I can't even make it through the day. I can't overcome like the Bible tells me I can." They continue to live in the straw house until the devil comes huffing and puffing and blows their house down.

The straw house is not for you. Regardless of how long you have lived there, you can choose to move. Pack your bags, overcome your emotional resistance, and call U-Haul today! It is never too late to change your address. Live in the stone house—the one that has the shield of faith as its door and the victory that overcomes the world burning in its fireplace!

Overcoming the Influences of the Past

Summary

- You must not only identify your hindering beliefs, but you must also identify their origin.

- Many of your hindering beliefs come from your past. Many people try to live their present and their future out of their past.

- You split open the events of your life and attach meaning to them. Many times, this meaning comes directly from hindering beliefs you have been holding on to for years.

- Your beliefs act as a filter for your life experiences. Two people can go through exactly the same circumstances yet respond differently because of their beliefs.

- People have a tendency to access memories from past experiences that *disable* rather than *enable* them, but you can train yourself to dwell on positive memories that will empower you for the present.

- You alone determine how you see things. Will you view an event in a disabling way, or will you see it in an empowering way? Faith is choosing to look at something positively.

- You must determine how you will respond to whatever happens to you in life. You will respond out of your beliefs

one hundred percent of the time. That is why it is so
important to identify what you believe and change the
beliefs that are hindering you.

• Your enabling beliefs are your protection and your power
to keep you from being squeezed into the world's mold.

• The devil will throw the fiery darts of negative thoughts and
circumstances at you, but you can overcome these
pressures by using your faith. You can choose to think
differently about the situations in which you find yourself
by meditating on the Word of God. You can choose to
overcome.

5

Changing Your Environment

Several years ago, we moved from Louisiana to Colorado. During that move, I had an experience that taught me the critical role our environment plays in overcoming our hindering beliefs.

When we arrived in Colorado, the first thing we did was unpack the moving truck. Much to my amazement, I did not sweat a drop. When I packed the truck in Louisiana just a couple of days before, my shirts were soaking wet. I quickly found that there is a vast difference between the humidity levels of the two states. I began to like Colorado!

The greatest benefit of my new environment, however, was not discovered until a few days later. I was rummaging through some boxes for a particular book I needed when I found something very strange in the basement. There were dead roaches at the bottom of some of the boxes!

Now, the fact that there were roaches was not strange. There is an abundance of roaches in Louisiana. The fact that they were dead, however, was very strange. In Louisiana, roaches are extremely difficult to kill. I did some investigating and found that roaches are unable to live in the Colorado environment. I was ecstatic! Now I *knew* I liked Colorado.

That experience taught me a spiritual truth. Those Louisiana roaches are just like the hindering beliefs we hold in our lives; they cannot live in the right environment.

You Must Move to Change!

God understands this. That is why so many times in the Bible He had to tell His people to move in order to grow and change. The story of Abraham is a perfect example. The Lord told him he had to leave his country and go to a new land where he would become a great nation (Genesis 12).

For Abram to experience the promise God gave him, he had to leave his present environment. God had to move him into an environment where his faith would grow and flourish. God knew that when Abram changed environments, his hindering beliefs would be challenged and defeated. God understood that Abram's *environment* was critical to his belief system. God wanted to change Abram's beliefs, so God changed where Abram lived.

A few chapters later, in Genesis 15, God promised Abram a child even though he and his wife were already very old. God gave Abram a promise that Abram found extremely difficult to believe. Many of us have found God's promises just as hard to swallow. We lie in bed in the middle of the night, tossing and turning in worry over our problems. A promise from God's Word comes to our mind. We answer that promise just as Abram did.

We say, "God, I know your promise, but this problem is huge! I know you said I could change and meet this challenge, but I just don't think it's possible. It just doesn't look like things are going to work out the way You promised they would."

God had given Abram a personal *rhema* word. Romans 10:17 says, "So then faith comes by hearing, and hearing by the Word of God." Abram heard God's word, so where was his faith? I will tell you exactly where it was; it was slammed up against the wall of Abram's hindering beliefs!

Hindering Beliefs Affect Your Hearing

As mentioned before, Hebrews 4:2 tells us that if the Word is not mixed with faith, it will not profit those who hear it. I do not care how many preachers you listen to, how many taped sermons you hear, or how many Christian TV channels you watch; unless you believe the Word, it will do you absolutely no good. It will produce no fruit in your life. You may think you are hearing the Word of God, but you are not really hearing. That is why Jesus warns us in Luke 8:18, "Take heed to how you hear."

Some people do not realize they have beliefs that hinder their hearing. They do not understand that their beliefs keep them from having God's best in their lives. They are not purposefully putting the spiritual brakes on truth, but their hindering beliefs halt any progress the Word could make in their lives.

When you hear the truth preached, whether it is the truth about giving, healing, or being successful, there is something in you that wants to believe it. There is something in you that wants to rejoice. You want to reach out and grab it. You want it to be true.

That desire, however, slams directly into a hindering belief you may have developed from some past experience or association. You want the truth, but you are unable to receive it. You have so much faith in your hindering belief that you have no faith left for the truth!

Breaking through Your Hindering Beliefs

God had to break through Abram's hindering belief that he would remain without a child for the rest of his life. That belief was entrenched in Abram's thinking. That is why Abram mentions his servant Eliezer to the Lord. To Abram, Eliezer was the only way God's promise made sense. Maybe Abram was thinking, "Perhaps God made a mistake! Maybe He was talking to the wrong person. Maybe he did not realize how old I am or how old my wife is!" When Abram mentioned Eliezer to the Lord, Abram may have been trying to straighten God out!

God knew the facts about Abram's situation—just like He knows the facts about yours! He did not need Abram to straighten Him out. As a matter of fact, He saw that Abram was the one who needed to be set straight on how the promise would be fulfilled. So in Genesis 15, God told Abram to go outside and look at the stars. God then reinforced His promise to Abram that his descendants would be as numerous as the stars in the sky.

When God saw that His promise to Abram was not penetrating Abram's mind due to Abram's hindering beliefs, God changed his environment. God said that Abram should get out of the easy chair, turn off the TV, and go outside. Then God instructed him to look at the stars in the sky. God gave him a new picture to consider—a picture that would change his mental environment. The picture God painted for Abram about his coming descendents was so vivid that it totally overshadowed the hindering belief that he would continue to be childless. God told Abram to stop looking at wrinkled, old Eliezer and to start looking at the stars!

God changed Abram's environment, both physically and mentally, to put Abram in a position to receive His word. Every hindering, disabling belief you carry is a product of the environment in which you dwell. A great part of your strategy for change must be to identify and change this environment.

Looking At the Unseen

The first thing you have to do to change your environment is to ask yourself, "What do I see in my life right now?" Paul tells us not to look at the things that are seen but at the things that are unseen. "While we do not look at the things which are seen, but at the things which are not seen. For the things which are seen are temporary, but the things which are not seen are eternal" (2 Corinthians 4:18).

You constantly view life from a certain perspective, from either rose-colored or dark-colored glasses. The question is "What do you see?" If you have the right perspective, you will see that your problems are only temporary; they are subject to change!

Do Not Be Problem Conscious

People who have hindering, disabling beliefs are problem-conscious. They are constantly focusing on the problems in their lives. They view their problems as permanent.

When the people of Israel were dealing with Goliath, they could not see around him. Every morning their problem was staring them in the face. When you read the story, you can see the hopelessness in their faces and hear the desperation in their voices. No matter how hard they tried, they could not seem to eliminate this problem.

....

God had to use someone who refused to view Goliath as a permanent fixture! David saw Goliath as a temporary inconvenience. Instead of giving in to hopelessness and despair, David opened his mental filing cabinet and pulled out memories of past victories. He remembered slaying the lion and the bear, and he told himself that Goliath would just be another notch in his belt, another feather in his cap.

It is absolutely necessary that you strive to see solutions to your problems, even when there do not seem to be any solutions. This mental exercise alone will begin to stir up creative ideas. As you begin to focus on these ideas, solutions will come, and the permanence of your problem will begin to fade.

Henry Ford put this principle to work with his engineers. He went to his design team and announced, "I want a V-8 engine! Build me a V-8 engine!" They told him it was impossible. They told him they could not do it. Ford was adamant in his response, "I want a V-8 engine, and I shall have it. You *will* build it for me!" They did too! When Mr. Ford got them to quit focusing on the impossibilities and insisted that it was possible, they figured out a way to give the boss what he wanted!

When my thirty-nine-year-old friend was diagnosed with cancer, my greatest challenge was to get him to see that the problem was not permanent. It looked permanent. When a doctor says you only have three months to live, it sounds permanent. But his condition was changeable. With the Word of God and with the power of the Holy Spirit, anything is changeable. You never have to be a victim of your circumstances.

Do Not See the Problem as Your Whole Life

People who have difficulty implementing change see their problem as their whole life. Every time you talk to them, they talk about the problem! Their life is consumed by it. It is humorous, for instance, to listen to teenagers talk about their troubles. It is certainly not funny to them, but as parents you can easily see that what they call a catastrophe is really not so bad.

•••

Many times we need the help of a new environment to gain an objective view of our circumstances. Our challenges are real, but there are also some very real solutions. One strategy I use to gain an objective view is to make a break from my current surroundings. In fact, as I write this chapter, I am enjoying the ambiance of a fabulous home in the mountains of Colorado. Friends allowed my wife and me to use it. It certainly helps to break the attention that a pressing problem demands. But even camping out in these mountains would have the same effect.

However, if all you do is change your physical environment, you will just take your problems with you. You must also change your mental environment by putting new words and ideas into your mind. You do this by reading and meditating on the Bible and on other positive books. You can determine your present level of effectiveness in dealing with problems simply by examining what you have been reading lately. If you are not carefully feeding yourself on positive, encouraging materials, you are bypassing one of the most effective strategies you have to enable yourself to see beyond your problems.

Your Problem Is Not Your Identity

Some people see their problem as their only identity. You are not a bad parent simply because you have a troubled teenager. I see parents who are under guilt all the time because they have a rebellious teenager. The guilt adversely affects them in all other areas of their life.

I have seen people who have failed in business or in marriage. They make a mistake and then allow that mistake to mark them for the rest of their life. They see the problem as who they are, and they are never able to cross the bridge to permanent change.

The Gospel is all about God's loving forgiveness and change. It does not matter where you have been, what you have done, or what has happened in your life. God is in the rebuilding business. Do not allow your problem to be your only identity, but ask God for help in seeing other positive areas in your life.

Ask Yourself the Right Questions

One of the most effective ways to change your wrong mental environment is to ask yourself probing questions. That is exactly what the prodigal son did as he sat starving for his own dinner with the pigs (Luke 15). The Bible tells us that he "came to himself" and asked a question. Whether you are aware of it or not, any time you are faced with challenges in your life you ask yourself questions. You may ask them consciously or unconsciously, but you ask.

I will give you an example. When something bad happens to you, what is the first question that pops into your mind? For most people, it is the question "Why me?" That is never a good question. You could ask a thousand more productive ones. You could ask, "What can I do, with God's help, to change this situation?" Or you could ask, "What good can I find in this situation?" The wrong question leaves you floundering in the quicksand of self-pity. If you continue to ask that question, you will never get out! You need to ask questions that will encourage you to seek answers.

The prodigal son asked a question that helped him straighten out his thinking and that challenged his hindering beliefs. He wanted to go out on his own; he wrongly believed he could make it without anyone's help. His whole hindering belief system was challenged when he asked himself some simple questions. He asked himself why he was slopping the pigs. He asked himself how many of his father's servants were doing better than he was right then. Asking the right questions will lead you to the right actions.

If you are having problems in a relationship, do not ask "Why me?" That takes your attention off what you can do about the problem and places it on the problem itself. Instead, you need to ask productive questions: "What is it about me or what am I doing that is making the relationship this way?" Or ask what you can do to change things.

Most people just ask "Why me?" and continue in their wrong beliefs. They never ask *what* questions. The real answers are

••

usually three or four *what* questions deep. When you ask yourself those questions, you will find out what you really believe.

The three most common problems we all face are related to finances, family, and relationships. In any of those areas, ask yourself, "What is it about what I'm doing that makes it this way?" Or ask, "What is it about my life?" When you reach a conclusion to that question, ask, "What is it about **that** that makes it that way?" You will come to another conclusion. Ask, "And what is it about **that** that makes it that way?" After the fourth question, you will get to the belief that is wrong in your life.

If a woman comes to me and says, "Pastor, my husband is treating me wrong," that is a pretty broad statement.

I ask the question, "What is he doing?"

She may answer, "Well, he doesn't pay any attention to me when I come in the house, and he always seems to be in his own little world."

I then ask, "What is it about that that bothers you?" After she answers, I will ask again, "And what is it about **that** that bothers you?" Soon, I will be able to see how she feels about herself. Once I figure out how she feels about herself, the next *what* question will tell me what she believes.

Asking yourself the right questions accomplishes a number of things. First, asking the right questions will cause you to change your mental focus. The right question usually begins with *what* or *how:* What can I do about it? How can I change it? The right questions will get your focus off the problem and onto the answer.

Second, asking the right questions will give you the right reason or the right motivation to do the right things. In 2 Kings 7, the Bible tells us the story of four lepers who asked themselves the right questions and were moved to action. Their city was under siege, and all the people were starving. The lepers asked themselves why they were waiting there to die. Why not take a chance and surrender? They might be taken as prisoners, but at least they would be alive.

By asking themselves the right questions, these lepers were able to overcome their self-pity and inertia. By asking themselves the right questions, they were able to come up with the right motivations to do the right thing, and doing the right thing saved their lives. When they went out of the city to surrender, they found that the army that had been holding them under siege had fled, abandoning its tents and supplies. They ate and drank and then went back to their city to share the good news.

I ask myself questions about the church I pastor. I ask *what* and *how* questions. What is it about what we're doing that's **not** attracting people? What is it about what we're doing that **is** attracting people? How can we get better at what we're doing? Instead of sitting around whining and crying, "This city is so hard," I ask myself questions.

Third, asking yourself the right questions will cause you to be renewed in the spirit of your mind. In Ephesians 4:23, the word *spirit* literally means mental disposition. Our mental disposition needs to be changed. Another definition for *spirit* is influence or govern. Your mind is influenced or governed by the questions you ask yourself.

You respond to everything that happens to you in life by asking questions. Your questions reveal your evaluation of the situation. Wrong beliefs always come from wrong questions.

You can see this with people who have a poverty mentality. They ask themselves the wrong questions. If you try to give some families money, they will refuse it. They are too busy asking themselves what angle you have. Your beliefs come from the questions you constantly ask yourself. You must change the environment in which your beliefs are planted.

I had the privilege of watching the Colorado Rockies' baseball team at spring training in Tucson, Arizona. Tucson has different foliage. A cactus looks strange. I saw huge cacti growing in the yards of people's homes. It looks like a different world. On the other hand, when I go down South and see the trees that are growing everywhere, I feel like I am being smothered. Different environments grow different things.

Many people said that the things Thomas Edison invented were not possible, but Edison just kept asking himself the right questions. Henry Ford was the first man who came up with a plan for successful mass production of automobiles. He asked himself how he could do it, while others were saying that it was impossible. He ended up doing it, and the Ford Motor Company is still in competition today.

One preacher told me that when he first started ministering and wanted to try something new, the following question would come to him: What if it doesn't work? He would always answer, "Yeah, but what if it does?"

I've had the same fearful question, and now I always answer, "But what if it does?" Your self-esteem, your self-worth, and the level you reach financially, spiritually, and personally are determined one hundred percent of the time by the questions you ask yourself.

My dad never had any life insurance. He did not believe in retirement. To a baby boomer, that seems crazy. Now we often hear about mutual funds, retirement, and 401k's. It is just like breathing. My dad grew up in the middle of the Great Depression. It was twenty-five years before he ever trusted a bank! This mistrust kept him poorer than he should have been because he always asked himself, "When is it going to happen again? Is that banker going to misuse my money?"

The Holy Spirit will give you new questions to ask. He will give you questions of hope. When the Holy Spirit starts working, you will start seeing pictures of things that are going to take place. Those new beliefs will start working on the inside of you, but if you do not uproot the old questions, you will not be able to change.

Here are two questions that will assist you to solve problems. First ask, "What is good in this problem?" Most of us would answer, "Nothing!" But you can always find a seed of advantage in any given situation, regardless of how negative it appears to be.

Trying to change an airplane ticket, I spent an hour on the phone with my travel agent. She told me, "I have never been able to change a ticket with this airline without being charged a change fee." I thought, "Now this is a fine situation; here goes another $150!" I told her to try anyway; it could not hurt to ask! She called me back later that afternoon, and not only did she get the change fee waived; she got a cheaper fare, and I got money back!

....

The other problem-solving question you can ask is "What answer am I not seeing right now?" This question implies that there is an answer. You can follow it up by asking another question, "What am I willing to do to find the answer?"

Here are more questions you can ask that will help you when you face a challenge spiritually or naturally:

- What am I thankful for in my life right now?
- What am I excited about in my life right now?
- What am I committed to in my life right now?
- What gives me the greatest joy?

When a friend of mine started helping me with prayer, the first thing he did was ask me questions. I did not realize it then, but he was locating me. He was locating my hindering beliefs so he could help me. He was asking me the questions I should have been asking myself.

The environment of your mind is influenced and governed by the questions you ask. To change your mental environment, you must ask yourself the right questions—questions that will help you think right and will lead you to change. Thank God there are other questions, besides "Why me?" Determine to change the environment in which your wrong beliefs are growing by making a commitment to ask yourself the right questions.

Changing Your Environment

Summary

- You must change the environment in which your hindering beliefs are growing. Hindering beliefs cannot continue to live in the right environment.

- God has to change our environment to get us to change. The environment in which you are is critical to your belief system. Part of the strategy for change is to identify and change your confining environment.

- Problem-conscious people have difficulty changing. They view their problem as permanent. They see their problem as their whole life and their only identity. It is the only thing they talk about.

- You must not change only your physical environment but also your mental environment by putting new words and ideas into your mind. You do this by reading and meditating on the Bible and on other positive books.

- When faced with a challenge in life, you must learn to ask yourself probing questions. Ask, "What am I doing that makes my situation this way?" Asking yourself the right question will cause you to change your focus.

- The environment of your mind is influenced and governed by the questions you ask. To change your mental environment, you must ask yourself the right questions—questions that will help you think right and will lead you to change.

6

Presenting Your Body

W hat you do with your body affects how you feel and what you believe. If you go into a store to buy something and want to write a check, you will have to present your driver's license. This should not be difficult because it only weighs an ounce or two. But if you decide to present your whole body by lying on the floor and the clerk has to drag you by your arms, that is a different story! It is much easier to present a driver's license than it is to present your whole body.

When we talk about the body, we are talking about this flesh suit that gives us the right to function in this world. When this body dies, you leave the earth. The real you goes on to heaven. Your body will die, be buried, and decay, but the real you will live forever. The heart of this chapter is this: The real you can control your body and affect your emotions.

When it comes to any behavior—positive or negative—you have a tendency to surrender to what your body wants to do. You have a tendency to surrender to your feelings. This is not what the Bible tells us to do. Romans 12:1-2 tells us to "present" our bodies as living sacrifices to God. *Present* literally means to stand as a third person to offer your body to God. Presenting your body means that you yield all your physiological feelings and behaviors to Him.

Most of us are willing to do this as long as the things we need to present are as lightweight as a driver's license. For example, we may graciously overlook a clerk's rude behavior at the checkout counter, smile even though we are irritated, and walk away without doing him or her any physical harm. We have just presented our body and made it do something we did not feel like doing. But this example is a lightweight thing.

• •

To present our bodies the way the Romans passage describes, we are going to find that sometimes we have to drag ourselves by the arm across the floor! We have to forcefully make ourselves do what we do not feel like doing. What does presenting your body have to do with change? Everything! If you change what you do with your body, you will change the way you feel.

Notice that the first verse of Romans 12 tells us to present our bodies as living sacrifices. This phrase means we need to make our bodies available. We are making our bodies available to *something* right now. Some people try to change how they feel by eating, by smoking, or by drinking. I used to wonder about the term Happy Hour. I figured out that this term is used because what you do with your behavior (eating and drinking) will change the way you feel (make you happy).

Let us say, for example, that your spouse made you angry before you left the house. Most of us will automatically present our bodies to our emotions. We will yield to the anger we feel by slamming the door on the way out, revving the engine of the car, and squealing its tires as we leave. When some poor, innocent soul pulls out in front of us, we will scowl. We are presenting our bodies.

I was at the local mall when I saw a man so angry that he backed up at forty miles per hour in the parking lot. He was going so fast that the sheriff who saw him arrested him. I could tell by what the man did with his body that he was obviously angry.

Presenting your body means taking your negative, emotional reactions to life and yielding them to God by refusing to let your body act them out. You feel angry, but you refuse to let your body act angry. You make yourself smile; you purposefully put a little bounce in your step. You do not feel like doing so, but you do it anyway. The physical presentation of your body in this manner will actually soothe your angry emotions. "Hey, wait a minute," you may say. "That's being hypocritical! After all, it's not the way I *really* feel. That's just not the real me." You are right; it is not the real you! It is your emotional resistance, and it will probably be your greatest hindrance to change.

We say, "Well, I'm not happy, so I'm not going to act happy. I don't feel that way, so I'm not going to act that way." Who said your feelings were a perfect representation of the real you anyway? Who told you to surrender to your feelings?

One of the greatest hindrances to change in your life is emotional resistance. Your feelings do not like change. They accuse you of not being honest when you try to do something by faith. But that is exactly what presenting your body to God is about—faking it until you make it. It is submitting to the truth, regardless of how you may feel at the moment.

Does the Bible not say that the "joy of the Lord is your strength"? Then what is wrong with acting like it is true? If you are angry, start smiling. Start singing. Start dancing. You will find that the passage is true; the joy of the Lord *is* your strength. Joy will rise from the depths of your spirit and actually change your current emotionally agitated state.

Presenting your body includes what you do with your posture, your facial expressions, your tonal patterns, your body language, anything that you can do physically. Controlling those things is not as easy as throwing your driver's license on the counter! As a matter of fact, controlling them is usually a challenge; most of us are very entrenched in habitual responses and behaviors.

I was talking to a friend on the phone when he asked, "Billy, are you okay?"

I said, "I'm wonderful. Why?"

He said, "Well, you don't sound wonderful. I've noticed that your voice goes down about four octaves when you are discouraged."

I started trying to change the pitch of my voice when I talked to him. When I started changing it, guess what? I actually started feeling better.

You can change how you feel by simply making your body do the right things. Paul tells us in Corinthians 9:27, "I buffet my body." When you start to do something new with your body, it does not feel right; it may even feel as if you are faking it. But if you keep doing the right things—acting as if you are happy or well—you will actually begin to feel that way.

Paul tells us that presenting our bodies like this is just our "reasonable service." He understood the way God created us, and he said it was reasonable that we act this way. When our children were young, we told them, "If you're happy, you need to let your face know it." That is reasonable, is it not? It is just reasonable for Christians to have a little leap in their walk. It is just reasonable to have a smile on your face. There is nothing fake about it; it is just your reasonable service! One man said, "We in America have made a romantic story out of being a victim." Most people today are victims of their feelings. Their feelings run (and sometimes ruin) their entire lives.

I am telling you today to rise above being a victim. Rise above those emotions that are keeping you bound and hindered. Feelings tend to be fickle, little creatures. Most of the time they have little rhyme or reason. What delights you one day may frustrate or bore you the next. So why worry about the constant fluctuations in your internal emotional state? Start with the outside and begin presenting your body. Start with the things you can change.

Do Not Deny Your Feelings

I am not telling you to cover up your feelings or to deny them. I am not telling you to think positively about your feelings. I am telling you that if you want to change your feelings, you must quit surrendering to them. If you want to change how you feel, you need to change how you act. Remember that all negative, disabling feelings point directly back to negative, disabling beliefs. If you will present your body like the Word tells you to do, you will have a significant impact on your beliefs.

Let me give you a biblical example. Isaiah 61:3 tells us to put on the "garment of praise for the spirit of heaviness." In other words, you can break that spirit of heaviness if you begin praising God physically. Some people do the opposite; they put on the spirit of heaviness for the garment of praise. It is no wonder they are discouraged! To stay depressed you must act depressed. By keeping your facial muscles, your shoulders, and your body looking depressed, you will stay depressed. Likewise, I guarantee that if you purposefully put on the garment of praise by jumping around for joy for just three minutes every day, it will change your life. It will affect how you feel, and it will affect your beliefs.

Presenting Your Body Physically

When we begin to present our bodies in physical areas such as eating, smoking, and drinking, we run into tremendous emotional resistance. For example, just try to help an alcoholic who does not want help! First of all, he must realize he has a problem. Second, he must want to be free. His body is addicted to the alcohol, but that pattern of addiction can be interrupted if he will cooperate. To experience change, he must change the presentation of his body in regard to the way he relates to alcohol.

Let us say this alcoholic always drinks at home in his favorite chair in front of the TV. First, he needs to stop drinking alcohol in this environment. He should make himself go outside in the backyard or go sit in his car to drink. Second, he should change the way he consumes the beverage. If he always drinks beer from a can, he should pour it into a plastic cup. There are actually many things he can change in this area: the brand of beer he always chooses, his posture when he drinks, what activity he performs right before and right after. You may say, "Well, those things you are talking about are not easy to change." They may not be easy, but they are simple. It just takes faith that it is going to work. When you present your body, you must do so by faith.

Have you ever made an appointment to go to the doctor when you really did not want to go? You knew you were sick, so you made yourself present your body. You did it by faith, knowing that going would make you feel better in the long run.

I had to come back early from elk hunting in the mountains one year. I had eaten some food that did not agree with me on that hunting trip. For a whole week I felt miserable, and I just could not seem to shake it. I could not get in to see my doctor, so he recommended I go to the emergency room. A doctor came in and asked me what was wrong. After poking around a little, he left and sent the nurse in.

The nurse said, "Take your clothes off."

I said, "What did you say?"

She said, "Take your clothes off."

I said, "I'm not taking my clothes off. I came in here for a stomach check. I don't need to take my clothes off for that."

After much argument on my part, she explained why it was necessary, but even after her explanation, I was not happy. I undressed, put on the gown, and crawled on the hard stainless-steel table. It took everything I had to get on that table and to lie on my side when I knew what that doctor was going to do to me. I did not feel like crawling on that cold, hard table and allowing the doctor to examine me in places I did not want to be examined, but I did it because it was good for me. That is presenting your body.

Present Your Body in Every Way

We need to present our bodies unto the Lord in every way—through our posture, our facial expressions, our breathing, our gestures, and even our tone of voice. Have you ever been around a person who has offended you? Your voice tenses up, and you are not quite comfortable. Your muscles tighten, and your facial expression changes. But you can change your whole reaction by changing what you do with your body. Begin to identify the little ways in which you present your body on a daily basis and start changing some of those negative reactions.

Present Your Body in Every Area

If you are declaring that your finances and your level of success are increasing, then you need to present your body accordingly. You need to act as if what you are believing for is true. By acting I am specifically referring to what you do physically. Do you carry yourself well? Is your posture the posture of a successful person? What about how you walk? The tone of your voice? How you smile? Are you animated enough in conversation? If you want to be successful, get around people who carry themselves with success, and start copying the way they present their body.

. . . .

Do It Even If It Is Uncomfortable

Clasp your hands together in front of you with your fingers interlocked. Notice which thumb is on top. Now cross your thumbs and put the other one on top. Does it feel uncomfortable to you? You have made a change that your body is not used to.

When you start to change your posture, your tonal patterns, or your facial expressions to respond to another person, it is uncomfortable at first. It feels like having the wrong thumb on top. I have been around some people who almost explode when they get mad. I tell them, "Chill out!"

They answer, "Well, that's just not me. I've always had an Irish temper." They stay in what feels comfortable and familiar. They want the old thumb to stay on top.

Breaking Familiar Routines

When you get in your car, you probably have a certain routine you follow. You have been doing it so long that you are not even aware of it, but if you get in an unfamiliar car, it becomes very obvious. The seat is not adjusted to where you like it, and the accelerator is a little stiffer than you are used to; so you react. It is not the car you do not like but having to do different things with your body. Physically, we tend to be creatures of habit.

I learned of this habit when I was waiting for valet parking at a mall. As I was getting ready to pull forward into the valet area, there was a young man in a fifteen-passenger van who began backing up very quickly. I started honking, some women on the sidewalk started yelling, and my wife started saying, "He's gonna hit us! He's gonna hit us!" Then he hit my car! I had a chance to practice presenting my body in a rental car during the whole next week because my car was in the shop.

Have you ever tried to get comfortable in a hotel-room bed? It is nearly impossible for me. When I was twenty, I could sleep on any bed, but now it has to be just right. I have to have three pillows, just the right covers, and a certain room temperature. Do not try to tell me that presenting your body is not important!

•••

Just as your body gets uncomfortable when you are in a different bed, your body goes into a certain sleeping position when you are angry. I do not mean you go to sleep; I mean the muscles in your face take on a certain form, your shoulders change shape, and the tone of your voice rises. (If anyone tries to get you to lie on a hotel bed when you are going through all that, they had better watch out!)

Paul said to present your body as a living sacrifice. Just as you have a certain driving position or a certain sleeping position, you can have a certain position of joy, happiness, and enthusiasm. There is a certain way you can carry yourself. Your natural driving position should be one of joy, happiness, excitement, and enthusiasm for the things of God and for your own life. If you have this pattern when something does hit you, instead of automatically getting depressed, you can present your body in joy. You might have to detour for a minute or two. You might have to get up, adjust the pillows, and roll the covers back for a minute, but you can adjust your body for happiness instead of for depression.

Try smiling. Now sing *Jingle Bells*. We have always thought that what we do with our bodies is not important. I can prove to you that what you do with your body is what causes you to be in the mood you are in. You could sing a few more Christmas songs, and you would be happy.

By your actions, your faith is made complete. James 2:21-22 says, "Was not Abraham our father justified by works when he offered Isaac his son on the altar? Do you see that faith was working together with his works, and by works faith was made perfect?" One translation says, "Faith without corresponding actions is dead."

When you begin to present your body, you dislodge hindering beliefs that are in your life. You tell the hindering beliefs what to do by telling your body what to do. You say, "I'm not going to react that way this time. I'm telling my body that we're going to do it another way."

If I have had a bad day, if my back is sore, or if I had a disagreement with someone, when I tell my body to raise my hands and worship the Lord, my hindering beliefs are all going to say, "No, we don't want you to do that."

What you do with your body breaks those negative patterns in your life. If you are going to change your life by changing your mind, one of the most significant things you can do is present your body as a living sacrifice. Notice that it is not a dead sacrifice; it is a living sacrifice. Your thoughts plus your emotions equal your beliefs. Your beliefs affect your behavior, and your behavior affects the results you get in life.

Do not allow hindering beliefs to determine your behavior. Do not allow those beliefs to tell your body that it is sleeping on a bad bed. You must tell your body, "We are going to do it this way from now on." When you start using your body as the tool God gave you, you can dislodge and break the negative patterns you have had all your life.

I found out that there was a certain way I approached the refrigerator. I had to break that pattern. My body was so accustomed to it that when my wife would remind me about it, I would get mad. She did not tell me that I could not have anything to eat; she just told me not to go to the refrigerator that way! She would say, "Sit down and wait five minutes." Or she said, "When you walk to the refrigerator, go around the couch the other way."

Smokers put a cigarette up to their mouth in a certain way. If I can break that pattern in their life, I can help them get free from cigarettes. But they must learn to present their body in a different way. James 2:24 concludes, "You see then that a man is justified by works, and not by faith only."

There are certain things (works) you can do with your body that will help you release your faith. When your faith is released, you can dislodge hindering behavioral and emotional patterns in your life simply by presenting your body.

....

Presenting Your Body

Summary

*   Presenting your body as a living sacrifice is a key element of change. What you do with your body affects how you feel and what you believe.

*   You can change your mood by changing what you do with your body. If you are unhappy, smile until you begin to feel happy. It will not take long!

*   Emotions are the greatest resisters to change, but you do not have to surrender yourself to them. They do not represent the real you. You can rise above the level of a victim to your emotions.

*   If you want to change how you feel, you must change how you act with your body. Remember that all negative, disabling feelings point directly back to negative, disabling beliefs. When you make your body act differently, you will have an impact on your beliefs.

*   What you do with your body can actually break negative patterns in your life. Use your body as a tool to reinforce the changes you need to make.

7

A Change Secret

One of the greatest change secrets I can give you is to find the right people to associate with and to imitate. In Galatians 5:1, Paul says, "Imitate me as I imitate Christ." Ephesians 5:1 says, "Therefore be imitators of God as dear children." One version says, "Be ye therefore followers of God as dear children." Paul wrote in one of his letters, "Follow me as I have followed Christ." *Follow* literally means to imitate.

Jesus watched and heard what God did. Then Jesus came to Earth and did and said what God showed Him. He tells us this Himself in John 8:28, "Then Jesus said to them, 'When you lift up the Son of Man, then you will know that I am He, and that I do nothing of Myself; but as My Father taught Me, I speak these things.' " In these verses we see a positive, imitating relationship between God and Jesus, between Jesus and Paul, and between Paul and those he told to follow him.

Realize Imitating Is a Scriptural Principle

God uses the successful lives of other people to show us how to walk in excellence. When we see people who are successful, we can, by matching their beliefs and behavior, be successful ourselves.

There are many teenagers who are going the wrong way because they are imitating the wrong role models. I always told my kids, "Be a leader, not a follower. Don't think that just because someone is a year older and looks cool, you should follow him or her. Find people who have their act together. That is the kind of person you need to study."

Put Yourself in a Position to Learn

Many people have a difficult time learning from someone else. They think the other person must have an agenda, so they are unwilling to receive anything. Paul scolded the Hebrew believers and said they needed someone to re-teach them the basics (Hebrews 5:12). He told them they were still in the first grade because they were not willing to listen to anyone.

You can put yourself in a position to learn by finding someone you can trust. Listen to this person, even if his or her opinion runs counter to your own personal beliefs. If he or she is successful and you are not, hindering beliefs are holding you back. A successful person's advice will help you grow and change, so follow it, even if it is uncomfortable and unfamiliar!

Ask God Where to Look

You may need help finding the right people. Ask God where to look.

When Robert Schuller was getting ready to build the Crystal Cathedral, his construction estimate began at nine million dollars. I believe the final cost of his project was considerably more than that. He went to one of his benefactors and asked him how to raise the money. The man replied, "How do you hunt a moose?"

Schuller said, "I don't know how to hunt a moose." The man told him to go figure it out, and he then would have his solution.

When he got home, Schuller started thinking about it and said, "First of all, I must go to where a moose lives. Second, I must learn the habits of a moose. Third, I'll have to learn what interests a moose. Fourth, I'd better be prepared when I hunt the moose." He took those four guidelines and raised millions of dollars for the Crystal Cathedral.

You need to ask yourself how to hunt a moose. If you are going to find someone who has been successful, go to where that person lives. The second thing you must do is learn the habits of that person. Third, decide what interests him or her. Fourth, be prepared when you go.

I once met for five uninterrupted hours with one of the greatest success authorities in the world. He came to speak in my church, and the next day he spoke to twenty thousand people at a large arena. Other people asked me what I did to meet him. I learned how to hunt a moose! I wrote him the kind of letter he would respond to. Not only did he come; he would not accept any money for speaking at church. When I met with him in private for five hours, I was prepared. I had a ten-page list of questions! I now have answers in my journal to all those questions, and the answers are an invaluable resource to me. In some areas of my life, I learned more from him in five hours than I had learned in twenty years! Get around people who are doing something right. Learn what they are doing and why they are doing it, and you will be successful.

I was amazed as I watched James Dobson interview Ted Bundy. In one part of Bundy's personality, he seemed like a normal guy, but in another part, he was one of the sickest, most demon-oppressed people I have ever seen. He had to have a sick, deranged mind to do the things he did when he murdered all those women. I am convinced he fed his thoughts with pornography to the point that he began to imitate what he saw.

When my friend was battling cancer, we found a little book called *Healed of Cancer* by Dodie Osteen. Diagnosed with liver cancer, she was told she had only three weeks to live. In her book, she gave us the recipe for getting healed. She showed us how to model her behavior and how to get what we needed from God. My friend did what she did, and he got the same results!

Some people have achieved a level of success but do not even know what recipe they are using. They are like my wife's grandmother. My wife asked, "Grandma, how do you make those tea cakes?"

Grandma said, "I don't know." Every Christmas we eat tea cakes, but Grandma does not know how she makes them.

Finally Grandma suggested, "Becky, why don't you come over and let me show you how to make those tea cakes?" Becky went and watched.

••

She asked, "Grandma, how much sugar do you put in?"

"I don't know, honey. I just reach in there with my hand and take this much out."

Becky had to watch her take some sugar from the bowl; then Becky put the sugar in a measuring cup to get the amount. Grandma really did not know the recipe. She was almost ninety-years-old and had been making tea cakes for eighty years, but Becky had to work to get the recipe.

Even after reading Dodie Osteen's book, some people still don't know the author's recipe for her healing. They still do not know what she actually did. They read that she meditated on the promises of the Bible, but she was not talking about meditating for ten minutes and then putting it down. She was talking about meditating in the Word all day long! When she talked about praying in the Spirit, she was talking about praying all day.

You may say, "All day? I have a family. I have to work. I have things to do." She did not care what anyone else thought. Praying and meditating, she locked herself in her bedroom and stayed there all day. Few people know what that is like. They cannot imagine what it feels like.

If I had the opportunity to interview Dodie Osteen, I would ask questions to discover her recipe. I would ask, "What was your thinking process when the doctor said, 'You only have three weeks to live'? What pictures were you seeing in your mind at that moment? What pictures were you seeing in your mind after you went to the Bible? What were you feeling? What were you hearing? What new information was coming to you?"

My son is a baseball pitcher at a NCAA Division One university. I told him, "When you get around guys who are successful and are making it in the pros, don't ask them how they throw a curve ball. That will help you, but there are other questions you can ask that will help you more. Ask them what is going on in their mind when they are on the pitcher's mound. Ask what they are feeling, thinking, and seeing. Get their recipe!"

Craig Maddox, one of the greatest professional baseball pitchers in all of history, has neither the physical stature nor the arm speed to be as successful as he is. He is successful because he knows how to *cut up* a batter, not because he knows the little tricks of the trade. He has success because he has a specific recipe when he gets on the mound.

When I write to preachers who pastor mega-churches around the United States, I ask for the tape series they were preaching when their church started to grow the most. I am not interested in just this year's tape. I want the tapes that will tell me what they were thinking and saying during their greatest time of growth.

Another thing I would ask Dodie Osteen is what beliefs she possessed at the time she heard her diagnosis. What did she believe about the process of meditating on and speaking the Word of God?

I told my friend, "I think the biggest thing she had that most people miss is that she believed in the process of faith. Most people do not believe in the process, but she did. If you will operate in the process of faith, it will work every time, but you must find that process.

So my question to this woman would be, "When you were sitting in your bedroom on the fourth night after the doctor gave you three weeks to live, what were you believing about the process of faith?" Most of us would be speaking affirmations of faith but seeing pictures of dying. I would ask what pictures she was seeing. I would want to know what was in her mind.

If you want to be wealthy, take a rich person to dinner and ask him or her these questions. What do you believe about wealth? What kinds of things were you believing and thinking when you got started? What images you were seeing? What were your feelings?

Some of you want to see your teenager come back home; some want to see their marriages restored. What images are you seeing? What are you picturing in your mind? What are you hearing and feeling? What are you believing?

I am giving you a strategy to discover the recipe. I know the Bible says that faith comes by hearing, and hearing by the Word of God (Romans 10:17), but you need to know what people did with the Word of God that made it work for them. You need to find out how they put themselves in a stance of faith. You need to know what they were feeling and believing.

When you are depressed and do not know where to turn, identify your thoughts, beliefs, and feelings. If you do that, you can turn your depression around. A lot of people are going through similar trials, but they are doing it differently because their focus is different. "As a man thinketh in his heart, so is he" (Proverbs 23:7). Discover their recipe!

I would also ask Mrs. Osteen how she presented her body. I know from reading her book that she put a photograph of herself on her wedding day on the table in her bedroom. She also put one of her favorite photos of her riding her favorite horse on vacation. Every day she looked at it so she could envision herself riding a horse. The doctor said she would never be able to ride again, but she said she would.

When she walked around her bedroom, her posture and the tone of her voice were confident. She wrote that she wanted to lie in bed, but she would get in her car and drive somewhere to pray for someone else who was sick. While every symptom of her body was screaming, "I'm going to die," she would go to the houses of people who were terminally ill and pray for their healing. Her body was screaming with pain, but she took her flesh, pulled it up by the bootstraps, and told it, "We're going to get out of this alive."

You can meditate on the promises of the Bible, but unless you get up and start acting like they are true, you will not see much happen!

I told my son to get around some of the successful athletes and to watch what they do. He asked, "What do you mean, Dad?"

I said, "Watch them when they sit in the dugout, when they run, or when they walk to the mound. Watch what they do with their body. Watch their mannerisms and their attitude. Whatever they do, watch them!"

Another question I would ask Dodie Osteen is what kind of questions she was asking herself when she went through that. I guarantee you that they were not about what she would look like in a casket. She was asking herself, "What will I look and feel like riding that horse again?"

....

Many people get depressed and ask, "Why is this happening to me?" They should be asking, "What can I do about it? What does God want me to do about it? What can God help me learn in the process of overcoming this? How can I beat this?"

The real question in the case of Dodie Osteen was not how long she could live but how well could she act until her healing manifested itself. She set an amazing example for us as believers who desire change. And thanks to her, my friend had someone to imitate, and it's working for him too!

A Change Secret

Summary

- Find someone you can imitate! This is a scriptural principle. God uses the lives of successful people to show you how to walk in excellence. When you watch someone who is successful, you can be successful yourself by copying his or her beliefs and behavior.

- Put yourself in a position to learn. Find someone you can trust and listen to him or her, even if the advice runs counter to your beliefs. A successful person's advice can help you grow and change.

- Ask God where to look to meet successful people. You must go where they live, learn their habits, and find out what interests them. You must also be prepared when you talk with them.

- Ask successful people questions about what they were feeling, thinking, and seeing on their journey to success. Find out what they believed at the beginning. Find out how they presented their bodies. Find out what kind of questions they asked themselves. If you ask successful people the right questions, you can discover their recipe for success!

- The difference between your successful and your unsuccessful endeavors is simply the difference in the questions you learn to ask.

8

The Anatomy of Change

The Bible has a lot to say about change. When Jesus was on earth, He changed things everywhere He went. Even in the Old Testament, God was continually trying to persuade the Israelites to change their ways and return to Him. And the Word tells us that the Holy Spirit is constantly moving among people to convict them of their need for change and to give them His help to do so. Change is a constant theme in the Bible. God desires for us to change for the better—from faith to faith and from glory to glory. Because of this, we can gain tremendous insight by studying what His Word has to say about change. We will start with a passage in Jeremiah that describes what it is like to be in a state of immobilization or staleness—a place without change.

Don't Just Sit There on Your Dregs—Change Something!

> "Moab has been at ease from his youth;
> He has settled on his dregs,
> And has not been emptied from vessel to vessel,
> Nor has he gone into captivity.
> Therefore his taste remained in him,
> And his scent has not changed."
> (Jeremiah 48:11)

Let us examine this passage line by line.

••

"Moab has been at ease from his youth;"

Most people will never experience change in their lives as long as they are at ease. To be at ease means to be comfortable. It means to be surrounded by things that are familiar to you. As long as you choose to remain in the familiar and comfortable, change will not take place.

"He has settled on his dregs, And has not been emptied from vessel to vessel,"

In winemaking, the dregs were the rough particles that were left in the wine after it was poured into a barrel. If the dregs were not filtered out, they would settle at the bottom of the barrel and contaminate the wine. In order to get rid of the dregs, wine-makers would tilt the wine from barrel to barrel and scoop out the impure particles.

In the process of change, dregs are the hindering beliefs that keep people from experiencing positive growth in their lives. If these hindering beliefs go unchallenged, they will contaminate people's lives to the point that people no longer even see a need for change. Just as dregs cause wine to become impure, hindering beliefs cause people to become complacent and self-satisfied.

"Nor has he gone into captivity. Therefore his taste remained in him, And his scent has not changed."

When people continue to do the same thing over and over again in their lives, it produces a kind of captivity. They become stuck in a rut. Ruts have the tendency of lulling you to sleep and making you believe there is no real reason to pursue change. (If it's not broken, don't fix it!) The truth is that a rut is nothing more than a grave with both ends kicked out.

A person stuck in a rut never overcomes his or her hindering beliefs and never moves forward to experience positive growth. Some people believe there is nothing wrong with that, but

••

in a Christian environment, being stuck is definitely not okay. God is not pleased when we are not growing spiritually. God is not pleased when our scent does not change. Change is supposed to be the lifestyle of the believer. Romans 8:29 tells us we are predestined to be conformed to the "image of His Son." We are to be progressively changing into the image of Christ, moving higher and higher in the things of God—not stuck in the things of us.

Sometimes people find themselves in captivity (negative circumstances or emotions) before they are motivated to change. Captivity can have an effect like that; it stirs up the dregs in you! But many people mistake their captivity for who they really are. They begin to identify with their negative emotions and start to say, "That's just the way I am." No, that is not just the way you are. That is not the real you. That is your negative emotion! You must look to the Word of God for your true identity. You must realize that you are what God says you are. You must believe what He says about you in His Word. If you refuse to do this, your scent will remain in you, and you will continue with no change in your life.

> " 'Therefore behold, the days are coming,'
> says the Lord,
> 'That I shall send him wine workers
> who will tip him over
> And empty his vessels and break the bottles.' "

Guess who the wine workers are? People like me! They are the apostles, prophets, evangelists, pastors, and teachers of the Church. God sends regular and visiting ministers to empty the vessels and break the bottles. He sends leaders to stir things up in your life so that the dregs can come to the top of your vessel and be scooped out. These people are not there to cause you harm but to promote your growth (Ephesians 4:11-12).

God sets these ministers in place in order to challenge you. That is why you must be careful that the church you attend is not stagnant. Do not be part of a church that is afraid to tell you the truth because it might upset you or make you feel uncomfortable.

Go to a church that has a growth environment—one that will motivate you to change.

Most people live and die in a non-growth environment. That is the norm. You have to fight the norm by placing yourself around people who are going to challenge you to grow. You have to stay around people who are going to tip your bottle. I did not say tip *the* bottle, I said tip *your* bottle! Once your bottle has been tipped, you need to successfully move through each stage of change until the change has been fully incorporated into your life.

Stages in the Process of Change

Stage One: Crisis

The most common changes in life are forced ones. Circumstances that we did not ask for are thrust upon us. Such unwanted changes may include a divorce, an illness, a financial challenge, or a job crisis. Whatever the specifics, something happens that alarms us.

The first stage is crisis. An unwanted event occurs. You receive disturbing information that upsets you. Things happen that you were not expecting. Usually a person will respond to the crisis stage with a lot of questions. What in the world am I going to do now? How do I handle this? Am I going to make it through? Why me?

Remember that a crisis may be a circumstance that is imposed on us from the outside (a forced change), or it may be something that takes place on the inside of us—something in our minds (a proactive change). We may suddenly realize that if we do not lose weight, we are headed for major health problems. Or unless we choose to further our education, we will stay in a dead-end job.

Let me give you a biblical example of a crisis. In Acts 6, there "arose a complaint" that some of the widows within the church were being neglected. The disciples, who had been handling all the daily affairs of the ministry, suddenly found themselves lacking. They were no longer able to do it all. They had to change the way they were doing things in order to take care of the problem. They had to go through a transition process. Ultimately, deacons were appointed to take over the physical work of the ministry so that the disciples could continue to devote themselves to the Word and to prayer. They successfully found a way to resolve their crisis.

Learning to deal with unwanted change successfully is one of the key skills that will make us or break us in life. The best way to prepare yourself for dealing with forced change is to regularly make proactive changes in your life. If you purposely force yourself to grow, you will learn the process of change and become comfortable working your way through it. Understanding the process will make dealing with the forced change easier when it does arrive.

Stage Two: Loss

Believe it or not, most people do not resist change. What they resist is loss. The truth is that every change in your life begins with an ending. The Bible tells us that new wine cannot be put into old wineskins (Luke 5:36-39). If you do, the old wineskins will burst!

When change comes, it brings something new. You must leave the old behind before you can embrace the new. Your old behavior, ideas, and beliefs are not going to fit any more.

When change comes, you can either deal with it and move forward or stay right where you are and remain the same. If you stay right where you are, life goes right around you. It changes whether you do or not. Jesus said that no one who has drunk old wine immediately wants new. We like what is comfortable and familiar. We believe that the old is better, and we resist moving through the change process.

Many times I have seen this kind of thing happen to parents. They desperately wish they had a chance to do things over with their kids. But that is impossible. My kids are in college now, and I find myself still changing with them and accepting their changes. It is tough. One of the reasons it is so tough is that I am constantly experiencing things I have never experienced before, and that is not always easy. I have heard moms say, "Oh, I just wish she was four again." It is easy to wish things were the way they used to be, but you can never go back. You can cry and boo-hoo all you want, but that child is never going to be four again! You have to change with the changes.

My wife recently asked me, "Honey, wouldn't it be nice to have a new baby?"

I said, "Absolutely not!" Old wine? No way. I want the new wine. I am just starting to enjoy being footloose and fancy-free. It is nice to be able to sit around in my underwear and watch television! Yes, the new is better. This does not mean, however, that I did not experience loss when my kids first left home. When they first left for college, I moped around the house and thought, "What am I going to do with all this time on my hands?" I was so used to their crazy schedules; kids were running in and out, and something was always happening. Suddenly I had nothing but quiet. Too much quiet.

People resist loss, not change. There are many different types of losses. You may experience a loss of security, for instance, when you give up the familiar and do something new. You may also experience a loss of control. One of the things that hold people back from success is the need to control everything. It is obviously easier to play it safe than to take a chance on the unknown, but all change involves risk.

Another loss you might experience is the loss of innocence. How many of you have ever found out something about another person that you would rather not have known? That can be emotionally devastating.

A loss of identity is another struggle. Many people have an identity crisis when they go through a divorce or when they lose a job. Some people have an identity crisis when they retire or when all their children leave home. Knowing who you are in Christ is what will sustain you if you face a loss in this area. Your self-esteem cannot be based on what you do or on what you have but on your relationship with Jesus Christ. Your identity in Him is what counts.

Along with other changes, you may suffer a loss of relationships. Perhaps the friend you once had has now moved on to another place in life and has no room for you. Or maybe you are the one who has changed. Sometimes you may feel a loss of direction. You just cannot seem to figure out where you are going! Losses of confidence or competence might be other things you have to deal with.

Even when you make a proactive, positive change, you may still feel a loss. For example, when you are born-again, there is usually a loss of old friends and old hangouts. You have to change playgrounds and playmates! Even though it is for the good, you still experience a cutting off—a separation. Remember what the Scripture says about the change that takes place when someone meets Jesus? Second Corinthians 5:17 says, "Old things have passed away; behold, all things have become new."

Every change begins with an ending. And that, my friend, is not comfortable. It is not comfortable, but it is the only way true growth can take place. Experiencing a loss is similar to experiencing a death. When you go on a diet, there is a loss of chocolate ice cream. You experience a death to that thing in your life. When losses come, you have to acknowledge them. It is okay to feel your loss. It is okay to go through that experience. You have to say goodbye before you can say hello! You have to acknowledge the loss, feel the loss, and move past the loss, or you will get trapped in denial. There must be a separation from the old before you can experience the new.

Stage Three: Denial

Denial is feeling the loss and getting stuck in it. You feel your hurt, but you wallow in it instead of overcoming it. It is very tempting to camp out and blame other people and circumstances for what has happened to you. It is easy to blame others for your hardships and troubles. I have talked with people who experienced a crisis fifteen or twenty years ago and somehow got stuck in the stage of denial. They are still blaming an old boss for their financial demise or an ex-spouse for their failed marriage. What is interesting to me is that many times the person they are blaming has gone on in life and is not even aware (or does not care) that the person is stuck. The victim remains bound while the offender goes free!

Even if someone wrongs you, you have to move on. You cannot stay in denial. The hurt or betrayal you suffered is real, but it is over. You cannot go back and change what happened in the past. That injury brought you the hurt; you cannot allow it to bring you death too!

One of the key ingredients to moving through denial is admitting what happened. Sometimes this is not pleasant. It may be hard to admit that a person you loved is really gone. It may be hard to admit that you really blew it in a situation with your kids. It may be hard to admit that the person you trusted as your friend has really betrayed you. But in order for you to release your faith and move on, you have to say, "This really happened."

God desires that we face the facts. He desires that we take a good look at reality. He desires for us to know the truth. That is what Abraham did when he was old and still childless; he faced the cold, hard facts. He recognized the fact that his body was as good as dead (Romans 4:19). When Abraham admitted the facts, God was able to intervene in his life. If we are brave enough to acknowledge the reality of our situation, regardless of how negative it is, God is free to move on our behalf as well.

Sometimes we do what I call the Tarzan swing. Thinking we are handling our crisis just fine, we grab hold of the rope. We try to swing over into the last stages of change without really processing everything that has happened. We say we are fine and do our best to act as if we are fine, but we are really still struggling on the inside. Eventually, the truth is going to grab that rope and pull us all the way back to where we started.

Others times we may vacillate between stages. We begin moving forward, out of the stage of denial, but then we back up. It is almost like doing a dance—two steps forward, three steps back!

We must move through all the stages in order to experience lasting change. The negative experiences we have in life will either make us or break us. The choice is ours. Everyone experiences unwanted change. What counts is our response to it.

Stage Four: Resistance

The next stage of change is resistance. This is the stage in which all your negative emotions show up. You have experienced a crisis in your life. You have recognized and acknowledged a loss. You are no longer denying the fact that something has happened, and you know things will never be the same. All of a sudden, anger, fear, depression, and guilt hit you like a ton of bricks. You cry out in anger, "Why did this happen to me?" You want to retaliate against whoever or whatever caused this negative experience. Sometimes you even get mad at God. You wonder why He did not do something to prevent what you are going through.

The experience of such negative emotions is just part of the change process. It is the chastening or discipline that is talked about in Hebrews 12. You have to work through these negative emotions. You have to get beyond them. Instead, many people become depressed and stay that way. If unwanted change comes into the life of a person who is not spiritually and emotionally healthy, he or she will move into this depression almost immediately. Even born-again, Spirit-filled people get stuck in this stage too often.

The reason many Christians get stuck in denial is that they mistake the negative feelings of resistance for the Holy Spirit's telling them not to change. They believe that because they are experiencing negative emotions, the change they are trying to create must be wrong. That is simply not true.

To move through resistance, growth has to take place. Growth can be scary. Many people have never experienced it. Because the negative feelings that accompany growth are unfamiliar to them, they label the feelings as wrong. These feelings of resistance, however, are actually a sign that people are on the right track. Even though your emotions may make you feel as if you are in a pressure cooker, the experience of these negative emotions is not what displeases God. What displeases Him is our resistance to dealing with them!

Our negative emotions will always point us to areas in our lives that need change. When we shrink back from making corrections in the areas that the Holy Spirit has made obvious, we are in serious trouble (Hebrews 12:7-8). Some people are spiritual bastards because they refuse to endure the chastening of having to work through the negative emotions that cause resistance. These people remain spiritually immature.

I once counseled a woman who had been married and divorced four times—every time to an alcoholic. I asked, "What is it about you that is attracted to men who drink?" This woman had some kind of hindering belief about herself that caused her to experience the same kind of unwanted change over and over and over again. If she would have been willing to cooperate with the Holy Spirit in identifying and changing this belief, things could have been different in her life. Instead, every time she experienced the crisis of a divorce, she would begin the process of feeling the loss, breaking through denial, and would enter the stage of resistance. That is where she would stop moving forward.

She would say, "I can't believe this. I'm a Christian woman. I go to church every Sunday. How can divorce be happening to me again?" Rather than pushing through her negative emotions of anger and depression, she would just start looking for a new husband. Somehow she believed that the next one would be the right one and that all the problems she experienced in her previous marriages would magically disappear! Getting married again was the only way she knew to get rid of her negative emotions (at least for a time).

This poor lady needed to endure! It is out of the pressure cooker of emotional resistance that you actually begin to experience change. This is the stage in which true personal growth begins to take place. Rather than get married again, this lady needed to push past her point of emotional resistance and allow the Holy Spirit to convict and correct the areas in which she had been blind.

Stage Five: Discovery

When you have entered the stage of discovery, you have finally looked at the past and said goodbye. You have attended the funeral of your unwanted change and have thoroughly experienced your loss. You have gotten past denying that the thing really happened and have worked through all the negative emotions accompanied with breaking through resistance.

The stage of discovery is a time to appreciate the past. You need to look back and remember the good things. It is also a time to reflect on the things that were not so good. Many people get stuck thinking about the good old days, but many times the good old days were not as good as we remember. I hear this all the time, even in the church community.

People say, "Oh, if we just had a move of God like they did back then. If we just had a revival like they had. If only the Spirit would move like it did back then."

We are having moves of God right now. We are having revival now. The Holy Spirit is moving all over the world today, and we are seeing people healed and set free. It is not something that just happened back then.

Hebrews 12:1 says that we must run the race that is set before us. Some people try to mark out their own race, but you must be able to run the race God places before you. You cannot go back and run the race of yesterday, and you are not yet prepared to run the race of tomorrow. You must run the race that is set in front of you today.

Discovery is a time of chaos. Good things are happening, but there is not yet a clear focus on where you are going. People often make a mistake at this stage by trying to pinpoint exactly where they are headed without taking the time to explore all the possibilities in front of them. I see churches and pastors make that mistake. I have made that mistake myself. I have told my church, "We're moving on to the next level," but I did not really know what the next level was. I did not give the people a chance to discover what was out there. Discovery is a time of transition, but too often we try to make it a time of commitment.

Two of the keys of being able to move through the discovery stage is to find out what is out there and what you can do. It is a time of new ideas and new energy. Spiritually you will never grow in the things of God unless you are willing to look at the possibilities. God is a God of possibility. He does interesting and unexpected things. There are some people I know whom God did not call into the ministry until they were in their sixties or seventies. His desire was to move them out of a place of complacency and security and into the realm of His possibility. They were brave enough to explore the new things God set in front of them and are now reaping the joy of those changes.

Stage Six: Commitment

Commitment is the stage in which you begin to invest yourself spiritually, emotionally, and physically in your change. You start looking at the place you are going instead of where you have been. You have firmly decided to follow a new structure or a new plan, whether it is a new job, a new relationship, or a new habit. You have firmly identified with the change. In your mind, you begin to see yourself doing what you have decided to do. You vow to make it work. You commit to the change.

Stage Seven: Assimilation

In this last stage, you totally embrace the change. It is no longer something you are thinking about; you have done it. You are no longer the same. You have now become something new. There is no going back. You have completely assimilated the change.

The Apostle Paul is the best biblical example of someone who completed all the stages of change. He came through the entire change process victoriously and totally assimilated the new into his life. In 2 Corinthians 7, he wrote, "Open your hearts to us. We have wronged no one, we have corrupted no one, we have cheated no one." In reading this, we must remember that Paul used to be Saul, a leading persecutor of the Church. Yet here he is boldly saying, "Receive me. I haven't done anything wrong to anybody." Oh really? Was he not the one who held Stephen's coat while the rest of the religious folks stoned Stephen? How could Paul, with an honest conscience, say that he had done no harm to anyone?

....

Paul so completely identified with the change that took place in him that he based his new identity solely on who he was in Christ. He really believed that he was a "new creation" and that "old things had passed away" (2 Corinthians 5:17). Paul could say with all honesty and sincerity that he had wronged no man because he knew that Jesus was made to be sin for him and that he had been made the righteousness of God in Christ (2 Corinthians 5:21). He knew that he had changed and that his old man truly was dead. He completely assimilated his new identity and the change God had brought into his life.

Do you want a nugget? Start seeing yourself in a place where the change has already taken place. As you go through the other stages, imagine yourself as having already made it through. See yourself with the victory before you actually have it in your hand. That is what Abram did. He walked around for twenty-five years, calling himself Abraham (father of many nations), and he did not even have a child. That would be like walking around saying you are a millionaire when you do not even have a penny.

It was during the discovery stage that Abraham started seeing what was possible. In Genesis 17, God took him outside his tent and told him to count the stars. He gave Abraham a new image on which to meditate. Abraham started believing that a baby would come through his wife, Sarah. It sounded impossible, but he believed it. It took many years, but he finally experienced the reality of holding his newborn son.

By the time Abraham moved into the assimilation stage, the image God had given him of being a father of many nations had become so strong and real in Abraham that nothing could shake it. Even later, when he was faced with the test of offering up his son Isaac as a sacrifice, Abraham still saw himself as the father of a multitude. Hebrews 11 tells us that as he raised that dagger to slay the very child God had given him, he believed that God would raise Isaac from the dead in order to fulfill His promise to Abraham. Now that is what you call assimilation.

A Challenge

As you finish reading this chapter, consider your current circumstances. Have you experienced a forced change? If so, ask yourself where you are in the process of change. Identify what stage you are in and what you need to do to keep progressing. Do not stop until you have totally assimilated your desired change.

Perhaps you need to make some proactive changes. Everyone has areas of needed growth. I want to be smart enough to tackle these areas before they tackle me! I would rather put myself in a crisis on purpose than wait for a crisis to put itself on me.

I challenge you to put yourself in a growth environment and to move toward the things you desire, instead of just trying to avoid the things you do *not* desire. People who have the most difficult time dealing with forced change are those who never choose to change.

Some people remind me of the man who opens the door and finds the devil standing on his doorstep. Satan proceeds to barge into the man's house and announces, "I'm taking your money; I'm taking your wife; I'm taking your kids; I'm taking your house." He then kicks the man out the front door and makes himself at home.

The man decides that he needs to deal with the devil and runs around the house to the back door of the basement, where he keeps his weight set. He rushes in and proceeds to work out for thirty minutes, giving it everything he's got. After several sets of bench presses, curls, and leg extensions, he thinks he's ready. Thinking that now he's prepared to whip the devil, he runs back around the house and rings the bell.

This story may sound a little ridiculous, but it is the way a lot of us act when forced change barges into our lives. We have not disciplined ourselves to make regular, proactive changes that will keep us strong and healthy and that will teach us the change process. When forced change rings our doorbell, we expect to be able to do a few spiritual push-ups and then cope with it victoriously.

Unfortunately, it does not work that way. We need to be lifting the spiritual weights of proactive change before the devil arrives!

Let me leave you with one more story to illustrate my point. Several friends and I went on horseback into the mountains a few years ago and decided to spend the night. We did not have sleeping bags with us, but we did have a big potbelly stove in our tent. Without that stove, we could have frozen to death. We took shifts to stoke the fire throughout the night. The next day we went down and got our sleeping bags. Sometime during the second night, the fire from that stove lit the tent on fire, and we had to run outside to escape the flames. We finally put the fire out by throwing snow on the tent. Literally, the same flame that kept us warm the night before almost destroyed us the second night.

In your life, change has the same potential. It can either be your incubator of personal growth or your oven of destruction. Choose to grow! Choose to change! Choose to do it now! Are you ready? If you are, come with me to the next chapter, where you will learn how to prepare yourself for proactive change.

The Anatomy of Change

Summary

- Most people will never experience change in their lives as long as they are at ease. If you choose to remain in the familiar and comfortable, change will not take place.

- The first stage of change is crisis. You experience a crisis when an unwanted event occurs in your life.

- The second stage of change is loss. You must leave old things behind before you can embrace the new. People do not resist change; they resist losses of security, control, innocence, identity, relationships, direction, confidence, and competence.

- The third stage of change is denial. Instead of moving through the change, you get stuck in it. To break through denial, you must admit what really happened.

- Resistance is the fourth stage of change. Negative emotions of anger, fear, depression, and guilt are often mistaken for the Holy Spirit's telling you not to change. These negative emotions must be worked through rather than resisted.

- The fifth stage of change is discovery. In this stage you finally begin to see the possibilities for the future. It is a time without clear focus and direction.

- The sixth stage of change is commitment. You begin to invest spiritually, emotionally, and physically into the change that is taking place.

- The last stage of change is assimilation. You have fully embraced the change and now identify with it. You are no longer the same. You have become something new.

9

Seven Attitudes Necessary for Personal Change

Having wrong attitudes can prevent you from attaining the changes you desire in life. Wrong attitudes hinder you financially. They hinder your relationships. They hinder your ability to make progress on your job. They hinder every area of your life. Your attitudes make or break you. They can propel you toward success or drag you to defeat.

What is an attitude? An attitude is what you really believe about something down deep on the inside. Your attitudes are determined by your belief system. What you *believe* about something in your life will determine how you *feel* about it.

When my kids come home from college, they talk to me about problems they are having in their social lives or with their self-esteem. I tell them, "I see you need an attitude adjustment." Then I talk to them about why they believe what they believe. I want to help them change how they are feeling about certain situations, and the only way I can do so is to help them identify their wrong beliefs about those situations. When they are able to change those beliefs, their attitudes change as well.

Attitudes determine how we approach everything in life. If we focus on developing correct attitudes, we will have greater levels of success. In this chapter we will discuss seven attitudes every person who desires positive change should strive to possess.

Accept Personal Responsibility

The first attitude that will lead you toward positive, permanent change is accepting personal responsibility. Have you ever caught your children doing something wrong? They have a definite tendency to shift the blame. You catch them with their hand in the cookie jar, and they try to blame someone else; maybe they blame you for making such good cookies!

Many adults suffer from this blame-shifting syndrome as well. As a pastor who has done a lot of personal counseling, I find that many people lose interest in transformation when they find out they are personally responsible for making it happen. This is especially evident with married couples who are having a lot of conflict; each partner wants the other to change. Neither one realizes that to see the changes you desire in your mate, you must change first! When I give this advice, the typical response is "Why do I always have to be the one to change?" You have to change because change is your responsibility.

Putting gas into a car will not make it start if it has no spark plugs. You can blame the gas station for selling bad gasoline or the car manufacturer for producing an inferior product, but the reality is that you need to take responsibility and have the spark plugs installed! People try to blame everyone and everything for their problems, but the truth is that in order for your circumstances to change for you, you must change. An old African-American hymn says it best, "It's not my brother or my sister, but it's me, O Lord, standing in the need of prayer."

Accepting personal responsibility is the highest form of human maturity. You are where you are due to the choices you have made. (There are exceptions to that, of course, because you cannot control everything that happens to you. Even so, you can always control your response. You cannot control the fact that a tornado tore down your house, but you can control how you react to it.)

In Mark 9, the Bible tells the story of a father with a sick child. The father asked Jesus if there was anything He could do. Jesus answered him, "If you can believe, all things are possible to him who believes." Another version of his answer might be, "What do you mean if I can do anything? All things are possible to you when you believe."

Jesus put the responsibility for the son's getting well right back on the man. That may seem unfair, but it effectively illustrates the vital part you play in changing the conditions of your life. You cannot remove yourself from the change process. You are responsible for doing what you can to change your circumstances.

If you are having problems with your teenager, you are responsible for doing what you can to bring about change. You can say, "I don't have any influence. I can't control what my teenagers do when they're not in my presence." Maybe not, but you can make creative decisions about how you are going to deal with their actions. You can make creative decisions about providing appropriate consequences. You can make creative decisions about gaining new knowledge and getting outside help if necessary. As you choose these appropriate responses, your teen's behavior will begin to turn slowly, like a large ship, in the direction you desire it to go. You may not be able to change the destination at the moment, but you certainly can change the direction. If you cannot change things inside the boat, at least you can influence the direction the boat is heading!

A minister discovered that his teenager was experimenting with drugs. He attempted to talk with his son but could not get through to him. The minister was at the end of his rope. He spent some time alone, praying and asking God what to do. A drastic answer came to his mind: He should take a leave of absence from his church and do whatever was necessary to reach his boy.

The minister decided to change their environment. He had been totally caught up in the environment of his church, and his son had been totally caught up in the environment of his drug-using friends. He made a dramatic decision to take his son on a shrimp boat that remained at sea for three months. Neither he nor his boy could leave the company of each other.

The results were staggering. By choosing to change their environment, he and his son were able to reconnect without outside interference. The son later said that when his father took a leave of absence, the son knew he was loved unconditionally. I spoke with this father before and after the trip, and it was apparent to me that he took complete responsibility for his son's problem. Yes, the son had to choose to change, but it was the father's actions and attitude of personal responsibility that encouraged the son's positive choice.

You cannot always control your problems, but you can always control how your problems will affect you. You select the direction you desire to go. When a person determines not to be swept along on the currents of life but chooses to swim upstream instead, he is assuming responsibility for reaching a chosen destination. You are responsible for your direction and destination in life, regardless of the opposition.

Remember that if things are going to change for you, you must change. You have to be willing to give up all your excuses. Some people go through their entire lives blaming someone else. They say, "I drink because my dad treated me badly when I was a kid." That may be true. He may have had a very negative influence on you, but now you are a grown person with the power to choose. You must accept your responsibility and quit allowing yourself to play the victim. Personal responsibility is the key attitude for any major change in your life to take place.

Take Personal Control

Next you must take personal control. Making a personal choice about what you are going to do with your life is the single most independent thing you can do. God gave you the power of choice so that you can take personal control.

We all have seen teenagers who try to model themselves after someone else. I recently encountered a young man who was wearing what appeared to be a logging chain. The links were an inch in diameter, and he had to lean backward to keep from falling over. Most teenagers want to do their own thing but end up doing the same thing as the rest of their peers! They are influenced by someone else's perception of cool.

Even adults in our society are constantly bombarded with messages to be or think or look a certain way. No one lives in a vacuum. Outside influences are perpetually trying to mold you. You must take personal control of your life and refuse to be ruled by somebody else's opinion.

Miracles can happen when a person makes the decision to stand up and say, "No, I'm not going along with the crowd. I'm going to do things differently." Against all odds, that kind of person will succeed. Your experiences in life are determined by your choices. If sickness attacks your body, you can choose whether or not to accept it. It may not be easy. It may not be automatic. It will not be without a fight, but you can choose. You can do the same thing regarding your relationships, your finances, or your own personal growth. You have a right to make such choices. You have more control than you think you do!

Expect the Best

The next attitude necessary for personal change is to expect the best. What are your expectations? Are they negative or positive? You cannot have the attitude of expecting the best and be depressed. It is impossible. Expecting the best is as simple as making a decision to see your future in a positive light.

Paul said he was "looking for the blessed hope and glorious appearing of our great God and Savior Jesus Christ" (Titus 2:13). He was expecting the best for his future. When you are looking forward to something, you have hope. Some people are looking for every negative, disabling event that can possibly happen, and they find them too! But Paul said he was looking for the best.

Like Paul, we should be looking forward to spending our eternity with God, but we should also be looking forward to fulfilling the dreams we have in this life. Stress comes into your life when you do not have anything to look forward to. It can be something as simple as going to Starbucks to get a cup of coffee, but it has to be something. Find something you want to experience and do it! Always give yourself something to anticipate.

I told a board member of a certain church, "The best investment you can make is to give your pastor something to start looking forward to."

He asked, "What do you mean?"

I shared with him how my church had sent me to Hawaii several years before and how that Hawaiian vacation broke a depressed pattern I had been experiencing for months. First, it gave me something to look forward to, and second, the change in my environment proved beneficial for me personally as well as for my congregation.

In the Nazi concentration camps of World War II, when the Germans were killing Jews by the millions, a professor by the name of Victor Frankel witnessed the atrocities first hand. He wrote about his experiences in those concentration camps. One of the things that enabled him to deal with such horror was the fact that he could imagine himself teaching again. In his mind, he could see himself standing at the podium lecturing. He could see his students. He knew escape was not probable, but the pictures in his imagination gave him something to look forward to. He began to expect the best for his life, and it galvanized his determination to live. He survived the concentration camps and made it back into the classroom. Later, he wrote the classic book *Man's Search for Meaning*. In it he shares things he learned from that terrible situation. Because he creatively expected the best, he was able to prevail.

We must have an attitude of expecting the best. The reason most people do not expect the best is that they have been disappointed once too often. Disappointing things happen to us all, but we cannot allow those things to cause us to hide our heads in the sand. Be willing to keep expecting.

I like to have three or four things that I am expecting the best about at any given time. I expect the best with my family. I expect the best with my children. I expect the best with my career. I expect the best with my finances. I write down my expectations so that I will always have something to be excited about.

When my friend was diagnosed with cancer, I encouraged him to start expecting the best by seeing himself doing something he really loved. For him that was bicycle touring. He enjoys high-tech bikes that are sleek and expensive. He and his doctor hit it off talking about the sport. As they began to discuss specific types of bicycles and upcoming tours, the focus was off his illness and onto something that excited him. He began to look forward to the day when he would again be able to participate in certain tours.

When a doctor says, "You have cancer, and now I'm going to give you every gory detail," your focus must be on something positive. Doctors do that because they do not want you to live in denial. But expecting the best is very different from living in denial. My friend did not deny that he had cancer; he just chose not to focus on it. Instead, he began to build an image inside himself of what it would feel like to tour again. He built an image of life and hope for his future. It changed his focus, and at the writing of this book, he has participated in several bike tours!

To develop an attitude of expecting the best, ponder these questions:

- What images am I presently concentrating on in my mind?
- What images could I focus on that would motivate me to expect the best?
- What choices am I intentionally making that ensure my present attitude stays empowering rather than defeating?

Do whatever you need to do to change your present attitude! When you see the positive results, you will be glad you did.

Be Willing to be Creative

Next you must be willing to be creative. Maybe you feel stuck or trapped in your current situation. You may have bad habits you have never been able to break. You may think, "I'm never going to change." You need to be creative. No matter where you are right now, there is a strategy to get you out.

Being creative is the most God-like thing you can do. God is the ultimate Creator. He sat on the edge of nothingness and told the light, planets, sun, and moon to be. He had a blueprint inside Himself of what He wanted this universe to look like, and He spoke out what He saw. God has given you an imagination like His so that you can speak out the things you imagine for your own life.

History is filled with people who dared to imagine physical things that had never before existed. These dreamers were laughed at by those who declared the ideas impossible. Many of those ideas became the inventions that we enjoy today, such as the electric light bulb and the telephone. They became realities because the inventors were willing to exercise their imaginations.

People have a strong tendency to doubt their own creativity, especially when they are trying to imagine a way out of their current troubles. But there is always a way for you to get where you need to go. There is a strategy that will enable you to make the changes you need to make. When you really believe there is a way for you to lay hold of the changes you desire, you will become willing to be creative.

My mother was a stubborn woman. All her life she resisted being pressed into someone else's mold. She faced many challenges in her health, and many times she refused to respond in the manner the doctors thought she should. She was willing to be creative. If the doctors told her she could not walk, she walked. If they told her she could not get out of bed, she got out of bed. I am not using her example to advocate irresponsibility; I am merely pointing out that nothing can confine you to your present circumstances if you are willing to be creative.

Have Confidence to Design Your Future

In order to experience change, you must have confidence to design your future. You have to be willing to call the shots. Remember the blank book? You have to be willing to pick up the pen and compose an ending to your own story.

Have you ever asked yourself, "What is important to me?" Many people are living their lives for another human being. Some men are still trying to please a father who has been dead for twenty years! To design your own future, you have to identify your own priorities and values. You have to determine the things that are meaningful to you.

In order to design your own future, you must not be limited by what other people think. If you are trying to make a change for someone else, your change will probably not last. You have to choose your own changes for your own reasons. You must want it for yourself.

Another thing you must do is identify your purpose. In a recent teaching seminar, the chief financial officer of a company asked me how to find his purpose in life. I answered that his purpose would be revealed as he identified what he desired in his life and then gave specific direction to those desires. Your purpose is your identified values expressed through your written goals.

When some people try to define their purpose, they do not consider their core values. They usually only think of two groups of surface desires. The first group they consider is that which will take them out of their immediate problems. The second group of desires is primarily money-related. Even though these desires are significant, people never go beyond these desires and reach down to core values. You have to discover your core values before you can identify your true desires.

To help determine what is most significant to you, ask yourself these questions:

- What would I do with my life if money were not an issue?
- What do I want my tombstone to say about me?
- What am I doing with my life that will live on after I die?

Your purpose becomes the strongest incentive for you to make needed changes in your life. Your purpose is like your physical appetite, except that your purpose functions on a spiritual level. Your appetite moves you effortlessly toward food, just as your purpose moves you toward the changes you need to make in order to fulfill your potential. When you meet resistance, your purpose will push you through.

Next, to have confidence in designing your future, you must ask for the things you desire. This may sound simplistic, but many dreams have gone unfulfilled because someone failed to ask. The Bible tells us that if we ask, we will receive (Matthew 7:8). That is a powerful formula. Many people go through life without asking.

One of the best ways to ask is to write out everything you want as precisely as you can. Being precise is essential. It is the

•••

difference between having and not having. Goals are like targets. Precision tells you where to shoot.

Most people take the shotgun approach when it comes to getting what they want out of life. They shoot and hope that they hit something. As a youngster, I discovered that it is easy to shoot a shotgun and miss! I went dove hunting with a couple of friends, and I shot two boxes of shells before I ever hit a bird. Doves fly extremely fast, and you must aim precisely to be able to hit one. The same thing is true of your goals; you have to define them precisely if you want to hit your target.

Not only must you ask, but you must be convinced that you can obtain your desires. Jesus tells us this in Mark 11:24 when He says, "Whatever things you ask when you pray, believe you receive them, and you will have them." You must believe that you are in possession of your goals before you ever obtain them. How do you do that? The answer is to use your sixth sense of faith.

Have you ever been desperately thirsty and gulped down a bottle of ice-cold mineral water? If you have, you have some idea of how faith works. The sensations you experienced when you drank that water were incredible. The refreshment you felt was unbelievable. Your sense of touch and taste became incredibly alive.

Faith works the same way, except that it operates in the spiritual dimension. Faith causes you to experience the sensations of having obtained your desires before you reach them. The sensations of faith are so real that you feel like you are already in possession of your goals before you actually reach them. As a matter of fact, when you do reach them, it is no big deal because you have already been experiencing what it is like to have them! You can apply this principle of faith to any desired change. When you experience the sensations of your change before you actually possess that change, you believe your personal transformation is possible, regardless of the obstacles you face.

Learn to Take Action

Another attitude necessary for personal change is learning to take action. Just beginning to take action is fifty percent of accomplishing your desired change. Many people see what they need to accomplish, think about where they need to go, dream about the possibilities, but never take any action. James 2 tells us, "Faith without works is dead." It also says, "You shall be blessed in your action." Change only occurs when you begin to take action toward your desired goal.

The actions you take must be harmonious with the outcome you desire. If you say you want to lose weight but keep visiting Dairy Queen, your actions are not harmonious. As a matter of fact, they are taking you in a direction contrary to where you want to go! You must bring your behavior in line with your desired change. If you can do this, you will be successful in any change you undertake.

Your actions must also be unwavering in nature. Harmonious actions amplify each other so that you become even stronger in the direction you desire. Physical exercise is a good example. The more you develop your muscles through constant use, the easier it becomes to do the exercises. You imprint the desired change into your mind and body by repeating the correct behavior over and over again.

Have you ever driven to work and then forgotten how you got there? The path to work is so entrenched in our minds that we arrive with very little conscious thought. Many areas of your life are the same way. You find yourself performing self-defeating behaviors as though you were on auto-pilot! The reassuring news is that you can imprint self-enhancing behaviors on your mind in the same way. The more often you repeat a certain behavior, the more ingrained it becomes. After constant practice, the positive behavior is executed almost unconsciously.

Adapt to Succeed

The last attitude you need to develop is adapting to succeed. There are two ideas you need to grasp in order to under-

....

stand this concept. First, if you do not enjoy the results you are getting in life, you must change what you are doing. As we will state several times in this book, for things to change for you, you must change. Someone once defined insanity as doing the same thing over and over again and expecting different results!

If you bounce a ball the same way every time, it will respond accordingly. If you bounce it harder or softer, it will give you a different result. In order to adapt, you need to watch the outcomes you are getting from the actions you are taking, and be willing to change your actions if you are not obtaining the desired results.

Second, you must be flexible in changing times. Some people do not change with the times, and they get left behind. This happened to the railroad companies in the earlier part of the twentieth century. They believed they were in the train business instead of the transportation business, and due to this faulty belief, they failed to make the necessary changes that would have allowed them to keep up with the changing times. I am personally fascinated with trains, but if I have to travel from Denver to New York, I take a jet!

Right now we are experiencing the greatest changes that have occurred to humans in the past century. The introduction of the World Wide Web and e-commerce will drastically change how we live, shop, work, and play. Companies and individuals that do not adapt to the times are sure to get left behind.

One of the purposes of this book is to help you develop the attitudes you need to adapt to the rapidly changing times in which we live. You can either stay stuck or grow. If you do not move forward, you can count on the fact that soon you will drift backward. If you concentrate on building the seven positive attitudes we have examined in this chapter, however, you will be ready to face any changes that come and will continue to succeed.

Seven Attitudes Necessary for Personal Change

Summary

- Your attitude is what you really believe about something down deep on the inside.

- There are seven attitudes you should possess if you want to experience positive, permanent change in your life.

- First, accept personal responsibility. You are where you are due to the choices you have made.

- Second, you must take personal control. Resisting outside influences and making a personal choice are the most independent things you can do.

- Third, aggressively expect the best. This will eliminate depression. Stress comes into your life because you do not have anything to look forward to.

- Fourth, be willing to be creative. No matter where you are right now, there is a strategy to get you out.

- Fifth, have confidence to design your future. Do not allow yourself to be limited by what other people think.

- Sixth, learn to take action. Just beginning to take action is fifty percent of accomplishing the desired change. The actions you take must be unwavering in nature and be harmonious with the outcome you desire.

- Seventh, adapt to succeed. Realize that if you are not enjoying the results you are getting in life, you must change what you are doing. For things to change, you must change. You must also be flexible when things are changing around you. Some people refuse to change with the times and end up getting left behind.

10

Obstacles to Change

Obstacles are the hidden roadblocks on your path toward change. They will stop your progress and cause you to remain stuck in a place you do not desire. They can keep you from reaching your desired destination. If you educate yourself on the common obstacles to change, you can resist them, go around them, or push them out of your way.

Living in Denial

The first obstacle that prevents you from making permanent change in your life is denial. You are living in denial any time you believe things will get better automatically. Things never get better by themselves. If you are consistently doing something wrong, you must first admit it and then fix it for things to get better. You will never be able to change a defeating behavior in your life if you keep pretending like it does not exist.

James teaches us to examine our behaviors in order to make our actions line up with our intentions. If we only talk about change and never move toward it, we are deceiving ourselves (James 1:22-23). We need to do something, not just talk about it. Do our actions line up with what we say we desire? If they do not, we must change our actions!

One of my favorite scriptures talks about how Abraham told himself the truth about his situation in life. Romans 4:19 says, "Without weakening in his faith, he faced the fact that his body was as good as dead—since he was about a hundred years old—and that Sarah's was also dead." We too must be brave enough to admit the facts about our present situation, regardless of how ugly those facts may be. Abraham is called the Father of Faith, but he told the truth about what he was experiencing at the moment. He did not pretend that his body was young just so he could say he had faith. He did not pretend that Sarah's womb was alive. He admitted the cold, hard facts but expected to see change.

If you are living in denial, you are not living by faith. You may think you are living by faith, but real faith faces things as they really are. It does not pretend that all is well when it is obviously not! You must break through any denial and look truthfully at the areas in your life that need to be changed. Are you broke? No amount of positive confession is going to help. You need to admit that you are broke and develop a plan to change your situation. You need to obey the instructions of the Bible concerning money and put some feet on your lofty prayers!

Breaking through denial is the first obstacle you must overcome to implement real change. Change can only begin when you acknowledge your self-defeating patterns. If you continue to deny reality, you will stay stuck.

Surrendering to Destructive Patterns That Only Meet Temporary Needs

The second obstacle to change is surrendering to destructive patterns that only meet temporary needs. So many people live for the moment, and if that moment happens to be painful, they look for a way of escape. There are many types of destructive addictions, such as drug and alcohol abuse, sexual addictions, pornography, gambling, and domestic violence, that seem to offer short-term comfort but will ultimately destroy your life. Negative patterns such as these will keep you in a continual state of depression. They may make you feel better at the moment, but you will not experience the ultimate reward of freedom nor be able to enjoy the blessings that accompany it.

Remaining in Your Comfort Zone

The third obstacle to change is remaining in your comfort zone. A comfort zone is an area in your life with which you are familiar. It is a place you know. When I go to a familiar restaurant, for example, I like to sit at a certain table. I tell the hostess, "Table nine, please." If my table is not available, I am pushed out of my comfort zone, and my entire dining experience is ruined.

I have the same type of frustration after my wife drives my car. I get in my car, and all the adjustments on the seat have been changed! I was elated to find a car that had two seat adjustments. I set one for my wife and one for myself, and now with the push of a button, I can be back in my comfort zone.

Do you ever get irritated with your spouse for initiating changes that move you outside your comfort zone? We want our meat and potatoes served a certain way. We want our pillow scrunched up just right. If someone has the audacity to disturb these things, even someone you love, you would almost rather leave the company of that person than make the change.

Most people live and die in a non-growth environment due to this attitude. Human beings are creatures of habit, and it is difficult to adjust to things that are even a little different from what we are used to. We like what is familiar, even if it is uncomfortable! We want to run the instant something comes into our lives that can bring us growth or change,.

Remaining in your comfort zone can be your greatest obstacle to change. Many times your comfort zone may even be unpleasant, but it is so familiar that you do not want to leave it. You have to abandon your comfort zone if you want to see change. You must let go of the old in order to embrace the new. This, of course, requires some stretching.

Have you ever done some kind of exercise and found you could not walk the next day? Your muscles were sore from being stretched. Stretching beyond your comfort zone will also make you sore. *Not* stretching past it, however, will make you stiff!

If you have ever tried to wear a pair of pants that was a size too small for you, you can understand what it means to resist breaking out of your comfort zone. Talk about being uncomfortable! In that situation, you only have two choices: lose weight or buy yourself a larger pair of pants. Do yourself a favor. Break through your comfort zone and make the changes you need to make in your life.

••

Desiring Change without Being Willing to Commit to Action

The next obstacle is desiring change without a willingness to commit yourself to the action necessary to obtain it. Every change has a corresponding action. Earlier in this chapter, I referred to James 1:22, which says, "But be doers of the word, and not hearers only, deceiving yourselves." You are deceiving yourself if you think you can get something for nothing. With every change, there is a price to pay. With every harvest, there is a seed to sow. If you find yourself in the same place after twenty years, wondering why change has not happened, know for certain that the problem lies with you. You have not paid the price, or you have not sown the right seed.

Some people lose heart when they hear statements like that. This generation has been afraid to pay the price for such commitment. Commitment is simply promising yourself you will never give up. The nation of Israel made that kind of promise after the Holocaust. The Jewish people said, "Never again will we allow anyone to do to us what Hitler did." They have kept that promise for more than fifty years.

Part of the problem is that most people do not develop a strategy to keep their commitment. You need a specific plan to stay on course. You may actually need to acquire new information—specialized information about the change you desire—to develop that plan. This information will help you nail down the details of your plan and will make it easier for you to keep your commitment.

Once again, let us use weight loss as an example. You can make a commitment to lose weight, but that commitment is too general to determine your everyday behaviors. You need to attach some specifics, and in order to identify those specifics, you need some specialized information about weight loss. You go to the library and do some research. You find out that people who eat mostly protein stay slimmer than those who eat many carbohydrates. You develop a strategy using this specialized information; you will increase your proteins and limit your carbohydrates. This

•••

specific plan makes it easy for you to exercise appropriate action and to follow through on your weight loss commitment.

Fear of the Unknown

The fifth hidden obstacle to change is fear of the unknown. Remember that we do not resist change; we resist loss. Perhaps we fear not knowing what we may lose! We would rather stick with what we know than risk what we do not know!

I have noticed that fear of the unknown seems to be especially difficult for people in abusive relationships. They are unwilling to change their expectations in the relationship because they fear losing their partner. Even though life with their partner is terrible, they fear life without that person could be worse! Due to their fear of the unknown, they would rather continue experiencing the familiar, even though the familiar is painful.

When I go out to eat, I experience a lesser form of this fear. A new dish may sound great, but I am afraid to try it. There is a risk that I might not enjoy the new as much as I enjoy what I always order. The old is tried and true; it is familiar. New experiences bring feelings of apprehension.

Several years ago, I went on my first white water rafting trip. I was not sure what to expect. The trip started in calm water, and we gently floated down the river for several hours. At lunch some of the rafters (including my children) were complaining that we had not gone through any significant rapids. The guides told them to be patient, assuring them that more exciting things were to come.

I became apprehensive as we began the second half of our journey. Within just a few minutes, we hit a major stretch of white water. I was terrified and hung on for dear life, wondering why I had ever agreed to try this. We finally reached calm waters again, and I was able to relax momentarily, thankful just to be alive! The other rafters were elated about how exciting the waters had become. The guide informed us that there was still much more to come.

Although I was still fearful and unsure of what was going to happen, I decided to try something different. I decided to act like

I was enjoying the ride instead of fearing it. I yelled and screamed with the rest of them. My animations were primarily motivated by fear, but I noticed that as I presented my body in this manner, I began to enjoy the ride more. I grew more confident, and by the time we reached the most extreme stretches, I was experiencing little fear. By the time the trip was finally over, I wanted to do it again.

It is frightening to venture out into the unknown. When test pilot Chuck Yeager described his experience of breaking through the sound barrier, he said he had no idea what to expect. His plane began to vibrate and rattle violently, and he feared that it might even explode. Rather than throttling back the engines, however, he increased his speed and found that suddenly his ride became incredibly smooth and quiet. He had broken through the sound barrier. He had pushed past his fear of the unknown.

What is on the other side of the sound barrier for you? Do not allow fear of the unknown to keep you from an exciting adventure of personal transformation.

Self-Criticism

Another great hindrance to change is self-criticism. You cannot make positive, permanent changes if you are constantly criticizing yourself. When you tear yourself down, you reinforce a negative self-image. Your mind tends to gravitate toward the images upon which you focus; therefore, this negative image only hinders you from taking the positive steps necessary for change. It is one thing to be aware of your deficiencies, but it is another thing to be stalemated by self-administered mental abuse!

As long as you focus on the problem, you will never see the answer. In the Old Testament, the children of Israel were attacked by poisonous snakes (Numbers 21). They prayed and asked God to remove the snakes, but God did not do so. Instead, He provided them with a physical representation of Jesus on the cross—a bronze serpent mounted on a pole—and told them to focus on that. When they acted on God's instructions and looked to the answer (Jesus), instead of focusing on the problem (the deadly snakes), they were healed. You must take your focus off the snakes in your life and put it on your ability to change. Everyone possesses inadequacies and deficiencies, but you alone determine whether you will allow these to cause you to fall short of your chosen destination.

The following steps will help you deal with self-criticism:

- List three accomplishments in your life of which you should be proud. (Notice I said you *should* be proud of them.) One of the cornerstones of the destructive pattern of self-criticism is always comparing yourself with other people. By constantly measuring your weaknesses against someone else's perceived strengths, you will always come up short. There will always be someone who appears to be smarter, healthier, prettier, stronger, faster, or richer than you.

- List three compliments you received during the last year. What strengths did other people recognize in you? Did you receive these compliments as facts about yourself, or did you just disregard them?

- Out of the one hundred words listed below, take the time to circle the ones that identify positive characteristics in your life. This is a great exercise in building self-esteem.

Loyal, faithful, fair, honest, creative, achiever, adaptive, gentle, kind, strong, persistent, thrifty, wise, successful, risk taker, dependable, astute, proactive, believer, positive, optimistic, encouraging, understanding, empathetic, giving, healthy, rich, sexy, handsome, aggressive, unafraid, finisher, musical, poetic, muscular, resolute, brave, confident, tenacious, trustworthy, devoted, consistent, cheerful, dedicated, competent, influential, resourceful, efficient, valiant, teachable, sensible, prudent, intelligent, discerning, scholarly, educated, reasonable, righteous, impartial, objective, candid, principled, pure, sincere,

goal-oriented, pleasant, sharp, agile, dynamic,
charismatic, energetic, eager, animated, earnest,
alert, practical, direct, certain, determined,
assertive, enterprising, agreeable, friendly,
proficient, qualified, skilled, important, inventive,
chivalrous, bold, tactful, discreet, sober,
considerate, unprejudiced, honorable, attentive,
courteous, refined, and grateful.

- Finally, determine an action you can take today that
will positively reinforce your self-worth. Only you
know what that is. It could be something as simple
as writing someone a thank-you note or telling your
spouse that you appreciate him or her. Doing
something every day to increase your self-worth will
go a long way in defeating patterns of self-criticism.

Mistaking Activity for Accomplishment

Obstacle seven is mistaking activity for accomplishment.
This happens when you engage in activities that have no clear purpose or focus. Many people stay busy but do not have a clear direction for their lives. They are mentally and emotionally running
away from change by burying themselves in activity. It is imperative
that you take the time to evaluate your current activities and determine whether or not they are taking you where you want to go. If
they are not, you need to stop doing them and start doing things
that will help you move toward your primary purpose.

I enjoy both playing and watching sports. Nearly all sports
have one thing in common; the participants are trying to reach a
goal. In basketball, for instance, the players are striving to make a
basket every time they get their hands on the ball. In fact, the basket for which they so aggressively aim is referred to as the goal.
Practices are designed to enable the players to do only one thing—
win the next game. Their activities center on achieving the skills
they need to be successful.

It is amazing to me how many people finish a year in life without knowing whether they won or lost. They think they achieved something simply because they stayed busy, but you can remain busy and never do anything worthwhile. Mistaking activity for achievement is an error no one needs to make.

Procrastination

The last obstacle we will discuss is procrastination. Procrastination involves putting off until tomorrow what you can do today. There are several dangers in allowing the habit of procrastination to form in your life.

The first danger of procrastination is that the longer you wait to change, the more entrenched a disabling behavior will become. The more entrenched a behavior, the easier it is to procrastinate about changing it! It is a vicious cycle. Procrastination is like a snowball going downhill; it grows by itself! You must apply all the techniques at your disposal to overcome this barrier.

To disrupt a habit of procrastination, ask yourself these questions:

- What can I do today that will make a difference in how my life turns out? You may not be able to change your destination overnight, but you certainly can change your direction. Identify small steps you can take that will be steps in the right direction.

- What resistance do I feel when I begin to take these small steps? Any time you begin down the road to change, conflicting and hindering messages will appear in your mind and bring you feelings of discomfort. These messages originate in your hindering beliefs. Identifying these hindering beliefs will give you the opportunity to change them. Remember that you can change your life by changing your mind!

- What do I need to alter about my times and means to overcome procrastination? Many people

●●●

use the excuse that they are too busy to develop a plan for change. They wrongly think that other people must have more time than they do, when in reality we all have twenty-four hours in a day. It is not the amount of time you have but what you do with it that makes the difference. You cannot buy more time, but you can put more value into the time you have. Others believe that the lack of certain resources (money, jobs, friends) prevents them from making the changes they need to make. They falsely conclude that their lack of resources keeps them bound to their current situation, when in reality their hindering belief stops them.

A final danger of putting off change is that you can simply run out of time! I woke up one morning and realized I had spent the majority of my adult life overweight. I tried to imagine what it would feel like to be my ideal weight. Then I thought, "If I don't do it now, I will be too old to enjoy looking fit." That thought was a great motivator to get me to initiate change. Do not wait until you are sixty-five and wondering where the time went before you do something proactive. Refuse to allow the obstacle of procrastination or any other obstacle mentioned in this chapter to steal from you the exciting opportunity to change!

....

Obstacles to Change

Summary

- The first obstacle to change is living in denial. You must face the facts. Change begins when you truly acknowledge your self-defeating actions.

- The second obstacle to change is surrendering to destructive patterns that only meet temporary needs. They provide short-term relief but long-term destruction.

- The third obstacle is remaining in your comfort zone. People have a tendency to stay in the familiar, even if it is unpleasant.

- The fourth obstacle is desiring change without being willing to commit to the action necessary to obtain it.

- The fifth hidden obstacle is fear of the unknown. People are usually afraid to change because they fear what they might lose. They are unsure of what will happen to them.

- The sixth obstacle to change is self-criticism. Everyone possesses inadequacies and deficiencies, but you cannot allow these shortcomings to restrain you.

- Obstacle seven is mistaking activity for accomplishment. Many people stay busy but are engaged in activities that have no real focus or purpose.

- The last obstacle is procrastination. The longer you wait to change, the more entrenched a behavior becomes.

11

Feel Your Way to Change

One of the keys to your success in life is intelligent management of your emotions. Emotions were created by God. They can serve you positively or negatively. Positive emotions are what put passion and vitality into our everyday lives. They give us the energy to do the things we need to do. Negative emotions, on the other hand, can hinder our progress toward our goals both relationally and personally. They paralyze us from taking any action to solve our problems.

God is interested in you as a whole person. He wants you to have feeling behind your actions. Positive emotions promote positive action. Negative emotions promote negative action or no action. If you allow the Holy Spirit to help you remove negative emotional patterns and to replace them with positive emotional patterns, you will find yourself empowered to do the things needed to bring about permanent change in your life.

In 1 Kings 19, we find a prominent story about a man who had to deal with his rapidly changing emotions. Elijah had just executed all the false prophets in the land. He had just had a major victory when Queen Jezebel sent him a message that said she wanted to kill him.

Elijah had been on the mountaintop. He had just challenged the 450 prophets of Baal to a duel and won. God came through with fire from heaven, and not one person who worshipped the false god escaped. It was impressive; good things were happening for Elijah!

Then a threat from the queen completely changed his emotional condition. Jezebel, irate that all her prophets had been destroyed, sent Elijah a message that said she was coming after him and was going to kill him.

Elijah probably wondered what was happening. What do you have to do to defeat this gal? You kill 450 of her prophets, and she still won't give up!

Elijah rapidly went from being a winner to being a wimp. He went from being on top of the mountain to being under the mountain. He went from killing Jezebel's false prophets to wanting to kill himself! The story tells us he wanted to die. Obviously, your emotional condition can change in a moment's time!

An angel came and ministered to Elijah. Elijah took a forty-day trip to Mount Horeb and hid himself in a cave. While He was there, the word of the Lord came to him. God began to ask him some questions.

Remember those questions that I told you to ask yourself? If you will not ask them, God will! He asked what Elijah was doing there. Elijah poured out his complaint that even though he had done a good thing in killing the false prophets, he was the only one left serving God, and now Jezebel was after him!

Elijah experienced two primary negative emotions in this story. One was fear, and the other was loneliness. God immediately dealt with both of these emotions. First, He dealt with Elijah's fear and assured him that if Jezebel and Ahab escaped from Jehu, Haezel or Elisha would get them. Then He dealt with the loneliness issue by telling Elijah that there were seven thousand others of whom Elijah was not even aware.

If God had not dealt with the emotions that were troubling Elijah, Elijah would have continued to overreact and magnify the situation, and he would have been paralyzed from taking any action. As it was, Elijah did what God commanded him to do, and his life was changed. Jezebel eventually met her doom with the dogs at the feet of Jehu, and Ahab died in battle. Elijah was able to take positive action because God helped him manage his negative emotions intelligently.

Avoid Overreacting

The first thing you need to do in dealing with negative

emotions is to avoid overreacting. When negative emotions come into our lives we have a tendency to magnify them.

Elijah blew his whole troubling situation with the queen out of proportion. He had just faced down and killed 450 heathen prophets; what could one woman do? Elijah overreacted.

When a challenge comes, a negative event occurs, or someone criticizes us, we tend to overreact. We attach the wrong meaning to those things. Proverbs 23:7 says, "As a man thinketh in his heart, so is he." Sometimes we thinketh wrongeth.

Suppose a man pulls his car out in front of you. You honk at him, feeling justified because he is doing something he is not supposed to do. Later, you find out he was rushing his small child to the hospital. Now you feel guilty for honking your horn. The occurrence was the same, but you have a different meaning attached to it. Thankfully, you can put meaning into things on purpose. You can choose to respond well. You can say, "I'm not going to honk. I'm not going to overreact. I refuse to attach negative meaning to this situation."

Look at Your Situation and Size It Up

You should look at your situation and size it up realistically and rationally. Asking yourself the right questions will help you do this. You can ask, "What will it matter two hundred years from now?" And ask, "Is this really the way it is, or am I blowing things out of proportion?" Try to get detached from the emotion itself and see it objectively. Let God speak to you about the situation. He will put things in perspective for you about your circumstances, just as He did for Elijah about his. There may be things you are not seeing realistically or judging rationally.

Do Not Deny Negative Emotions

When you deny a situation, you stick your head in the sand like an ostrich and pretend that the situation does not exist or that it does not bother you. Some people try to deny their negative emotions. They do not want anyone to know what they are feeling, so they refuse to admit it, even to themselves. You should not magnify your emotions, but you must not deny them either.

If you have a troubled teenager, if you are going through a financial crisis, or if you are experiencing marital problems, you feel fear. It is this fear that causes you to shut down emotionally. You deny that the situation is happening. Because you deny it, you do not take any positive action to change.

Develop a Pattern of Responding Correctly

Emotions were given to you by God. One of the reasons God gave you emotions is to make you who you are. Emotions make you unique. Emotions that are used correctly enable you, but emotions that are used incorrectly disable you. Emotions can empower you, or they can paralyze you.

You need to develop a pattern of responding correctly to negative emotions. Identify the emotions with which you struggle and develop a strategy to overcome them. When God spoke to Elijah, God dealt very specifically with Elijah's negative emotions of fear and loneliness. God told Elijah what action to take to overcome those feelings.

The primary negative emotions most people have are fear, anger, disappointment, guilt, depression, and inadequacy. Usually they struggle with these emotions due to past hurts that need resolution. People continue to allow these hurts of the past to speak into their present and their future by continually opening the negative memory file in their minds. Everywhere they go, they spew hurt. They are frequently found dumping their emotional mess onto other people.

If you are close to a person who struggles with negative emotions or if you are that person, take action! You must say to these struggling people (or to yourself), "I love you and care for you, but you can't remain a victim." If you pat their back and try to comfort them, you are doing nothing to help them. Ask them *what* and *how* questions until you get to the root of their false belief. Then help them change their life by changing their mind!

Use Negative Emotions as Indicators, Not as Captivators

You can learn to use your negative emotions as indicators, as triggers to help you identify your wrong beliefs. Negative emotions always point to beliefs that are not right. There is a reason why you feel afraid. There is a reason why you feel angry. There is a reason why you feel hurt. Emotions help you identify the places you need to change. For example, if you are afraid, the emotion of fear comes directly from a wrong belief. Look beyond the emotion to identify the belief that is causing you to be afraid or angry.

Negative emotions will also point to wrong behavior. God twice asked Elijah, "What are you doing here?" God was trying to help Elijah identify his behavior. God was using Elijah's negative emotions as indicators that something was wrong in Elijah's life. The question also referred to his behavior. Elijah's negative emotions had paralyzed him from making any further progress with his goals. He was too busy hiding! God was challenging him to be out doing what he was supposed to be doing. He should be anointing people. God told him not to just sit on the mountain—go!

Use Your Positive Emotions as Motivators

Ask the Holy Spirit to empower you with positive emotions. The Bible calls the positive emotions we desire the fruit of the Spirit. "But the fruit of the Spirit is love, joy, peace, longsuffering, kindness, goodness, faithfulness, gentleness, self-control. Against such there is no law" (Galatians 5:22-23).

I want you to notice that all the fruits can be both emotions and behaviors. They are emotions in some situations and behaviors in others. Love is an emotion, but it is also an action. Joy is an emotion, but it is also an action. Peace is primarily an emotion, but it can also be an action. These fruits are expressed inwardly as our emotions and outwardly as our actions. We are strengthened when we allow these positive emotions to empower us to reach our dreams, to treat others with compassion, and to always see life in positive terms.

Change Your Focus or Change Your Actions

Remember that negative emotions always point to hindering beliefs. Asking the right questions will change your focus and help you identify your negative beliefs. Below are three questions you can ask when experiencing negative emotions:

- What can I learn from experiencing this negative emotion right now?
- What is this emotion trying to reveal to me about me?
- What beliefs do I need to change?

There are two primary ways you can change your emotions. First, you can change your focus. If you are depressed, for instance, it is because you are mentally focusing on an image that brings depression. If you are in fear, you are mentally focusing on pictures that bring fear. But you have the power to choose what you will focus on. Ask the Holy Spirit to give you a positive image that will replace your negative one.

The second way you can change your emotions is by changing your actions. Positive emotions empower you to positive actions, but positive actions will also inspire positive emotions. They feed off each other. If a couple that has been married for ten years wants to feel romance again, the people need to act romantically, and the feelings will return.

God wants you to be blessed with both the positive action and the feeling behind that action.

Feel Your Way to Change

Summary

- Avoid overreacting to negative emotions. People have a tendency to go to extremes by either magnifying negative emotions or by denying them all together. The intelligent management of emotions is a key to success in life.

- Look at each negative situation or problem and size it up realistically and rationally. Will it matter two hundred years from now? Is this really the way it is, or am I blowing things out of proportion?

- Develop a pattern of responding correctly to negative emotions. Identify which ones you deal with the most and develop a strategy to overcome them.

- Use your negative emotions as indicators, not as captivators. The emotions of fear, anger, guilt, and depression always point directly back to hindering beliefs you need to change.

- Use your positive emotions as motivators. Let the Holy Spirit fill you with faith, hope, and love. These will propel you to positive action. Positive emotions give you the energy to do what you need to do.

- You can change your emotions by changing your focus or your actions. You can change your actions by changing your beliefs.

12

Releasing the Forces of Change

There are two forces that motivate us each day. The first force is a desire to move away from pain. If I held a burning flame under your hand, you would move quickly. It is a natural instinct to move away from pain. It is also the motivator that causes us to seek short-term pleasures that bring negative long-term consequences. Drugs, alcohol, and other harmful behaviors are prevalent in our society because people want to move away from the pain in their lives. They acquire negative addictions as a way of escape. The second motivator is a desire to move toward gain or pleasure. I want you to understand that everything you do is for one of these two reasons.

God created two places that are perfect matches for these two motivators. Those places are heaven and hell. The highest motive for getting saved and for coming to God is the thought of gaining heaven, but the other reason we serve Him is our desire to avoid hell! Because He made us, God understands how we function better than any psychologist does.

Moving Away from and Moving Toward

Some people are more inclined to move away from things. The only reason they do anything is to move away from something. Some churches have learned to use this motivator to make people feel guilty, but I learned a long time ago that you cannot pastor a healthy church by producing guilt in the people that come.

Many people move toward things. When women go shopping for a new dress they are moving toward something. There is a motivator. There is a glint in their eyes, there is a purpose on their face, and no one better get in their way. Men act the same way in the fishing shop! Shopping is a *moving-toward* motivator. You are moving toward gain and pleasure. We take action to move toward something.

The Holy Spirit is the change agent. He helps us move away from the hindering beliefs in our lives and move toward empowering beliefs. Jesus described the Holy Spirit in John 16. The Holy Spirit is God's agent of change. He convicts us of sin; He convinces us that we are missing the mark. The word *sin* literally means missing the mark. Sin is not just the wrong things we do. It includes the wrong things, but it is not limited to them. The Holy Spirit convinces us of where we are missing the mark and of our hindering beliefs. If we will take the time to listen to the Holy Spirit, He will reveal things to us that we need to know about the way we think.

Many times past voices, past experiences, and past associations are the loudest voices we hear, but these voices are not the Word of God! We can choose not to listen to them. We know the voices we hear are God's, the devil's, and our own. We think we give God one-third, the devil one-third, and ourselves one-third. According to Mark 4, the good seed (good voices) only finds good ground (our minds) about twenty-five percent of the time! That leaves seventy-five percent up for grabs!

Sorrow That Leads to Repentance and Hope That Leads to Faith

The Holy Spirit has two primary forces that He uses to motivate you to change. The first one He produces in you is the sorrow that leads to repentance. Have you ever been at a place in your life where you have said, "I've had it! I'm tired of getting kicked around. I'm tired of being beat up. I'm tired of my life running this way. I'm telling you that I've HAD IT!" That is the Holy Spirit's producing in you the sorrow that leads to repentance. He is helping you become sorry for letting the circumstances of life push you around.

There is nothing in existence that can stop the human will when it says, "I've had it!" When you say you've had it and let God work through your sorrow, you will experience change. You will be led away from pain. You will have changed your mind about the circumstance. You will not put up with it any longer. You will have changed it by putting your foot down and by saying emphatically, "I've had it."

My wife once repented over her nail color. She had a certain nail color when she came home from the nail parlor and asked me, "Honey, do you like this color?"

I looked at it and thought, "If I tell her I like it, I will be in trouble, and if I tell her I don't, I will be in trouble." So I said, "Let me look at it again." So I looked at it again. Then I said what the prophet said to Saul, "Just go and do as it seems good to you." So she went and did as it seemed good to her. She paid another forty dollars and had it changed! She repented; she changed her mind.

You say, "I can't change that quickly or easily." Actually, it is just as easy to change an entrenched habit as it is to change a nail color if you allow the sorrow that leads to repentance to begin working in your life. We have thought inaccurately that change takes a long time. Why do you think the Holy Spirit is here? He is here so that quick and effective change is possible.

The Holy Spirit is here as an agent of God to teach us to change. There is not a God-fearing, Bible-believing Christian anywhere who would not say the Holy Spirit is the teacher of the Church. Well, who is the Church? The Church is you and I! And He is teaching us. He is showing us things about Jesus so we become Christ-like. We need to let Him to show us where we need change by pointing out those hindering beliefs in our lives.

The second way the Holy Spirit works in us for change is by the hope that leads to faith. Romans 15:13 says, "Now may the God of hope fill you with all joy and peace in believing, that you may abound in hope by the power of the Holy Spirit." The opposite of sorrow is joy. The Holy Spirit not only tells us what to move away from; He gives us the ability to move toward the positive too!

When it comes to change, most of us say, "Oh, I want a change in my life. God, please give me change in my life." Why do we keep asking God for it? Are we powerless? Are we out here by ourselves? No! The Holy Spirit lives inside of us. The Bible tells

• •

us the weapons of our warfare are not carnal—not natural—but supernatural.

So the Holy Spirit will give you sorrow, which leads to the changing of your mind, but it is a good sorrow that says, "You can change, you will change, and you will want to change." Before this, you were just entertaining your hindering beliefs. You were having a tea party with them! When the Spirit of God begins to speak to you, however, you quit serving tea because you begin to feel uncomfortable. He begins to stir within you a holy dissatisfaction. He will paint a picture on the inside of you, and you will start seeing yourself coming out of your mess!

When real change starts coming to your life, there will be sorrow that leads to repentance, and there will be hope that leads to faith. The Holy Spirit will use both these motivators. If all you have is sorrow that leads to repentance, you may change your mind, but you will not know what to do next! Hope that leads you to faith gives you something to do! Hebrews 11:6 tells us that He is "a rewarder of those who diligently seek Him." God will bring you into positive areas of change that you never dreamed were possible.

When we moved to Colorado, we basically started over by renting a home. My wife would come to me and say, "Honey, I need my own home." She would literally weep over not owning a house. I did not understand. Men can live in a tent; a woman wants to live in a castle.

She started praying for me, and the Holy Spirit started talking. He started giving me the sorrow that leads to repentance. Every time I would get around people who owned their own home, I started grieving. I was changing my mind about the importance of having our own place.

The Holy Spirit also motivated my wife. He gave her the hope that leads to faith. She wrote down a description of the kind of house she wanted. That gave her hope! She got excited about her description! She actually started moving toward our home in her mind. The image of a new house became so vivid to her that God gave her a new house! And it was quite a bit larger than the one she was dreaming about! We built it ourselves; it was new. No one had lived in it. She was able to have it built the way she wanted it. She wanted it this way. She wanted it that way. She wanted this and that. I thought, "I didn't know a woman could have so many details!" The Spirit of God led her to hope, the hope that leads to faith.

The Holy Spirit gives you the hope that leads to faith too. You can change. What pictures are you seeing? Let the Holy Spirit give you new pictures because hope that leads to faith always produces pictures. You will start seeing something. You will start seeing that teenager come home; you will start seeing that habit break off. You will start seeing those positive changes in your personality that you have always wanted to make. You have to *see* it before you actually *have* it; that is how change works.

Now that you understand the two forces the Holy Spirit uses, write down three areas of your life in which you would like to see change. Ask this question: What specifically about those areas of my life needs to be changed? It is one thing to say, "I need more money." It is another thing to get specific about it. God always works in specifics.

Next, write down three actions you can take that will help you achieve those things you wrote down. You say, "Why is it necessary to write down the actions I will take?" Because God will not turn a car that is sitting still! Your car must be moving in order to turn it. You have to be willing to say, "Lord, I'm willing to obey; you just show me." You cannot turn a car unless it has some motion. People are the same way. God is trying to help us change, but we are sitting still in the parking lot with the brakes on.

Next, ask yourself these telling questions: Why have I not taken these actions that I just wrote down? What would I lose or gain, short-term or long-term, by taking these actions?

Also ask yourself what you are gaining by allowing this behavior in your life. If it is a behavior or a circumstance that you want to change, what are you gaining by allowing this behavior to continue? I would ask myself what will happen in the long-term if I don't change now.

We can change, and we can change now. We are not limited to the world's timing. We have the forces of the Holy Spirit working in us. If we understand what those forces are—sorrow that leads to repentance and hope that leads to faith—we can determine to cooperate with them, and permanent change can come.

....

Releasing the Forces of Change

Summary

- The first force that motivates people to change is a natural instinct to move away from pain.

- The second force that motivates people to change is the desire to move toward gain or pleasure.

- God will help you move away from hindering beliefs by enabling you to pull them down and to destroy them permanently.

- The Holy Sprit will convict you of sin but will not cause you to feel guilty. His desire is to show you where you are missing the mark by helping you identify your hindering beliefs. If you can identify them, you can change them!

- The Holy Spirit uses two forces to help you change: sorrow that leads to repentance and hope that leads to faith.

- Repentance means that you change your mind about something. When you change your thoughts about something, you will correspondingly change your actions.

- The Holy Spirit will give you pictures of yourself changed. He will paint vivid pictures inside you of what you can be. When you cooperate with Him by dwelling on those pictures, you are drawn to do the things you need to do to bring permanent change into your life.

13

The One Thing that Remains the Same— Change!

People are looking for change. I believe that the United States of America is on the verge of a spiritual awakening. The people are hungry. I welcome that awakening, but at the same time, I am concerned. After over twenty years of ministry experience, I know how difficult it can be for people to change. It is not something that just happens.

What I have found is that most people like to stay in situations that are comfortable and familiar, even if those situations are unpleasant. People do not like the risk of venturing out into the darkness of the unknown, even if what is out there has the potential to improve life. Change is always risky, but we have to learn to take that risk. To stay where you are is to grow stagnant and die.

Change is a process that anyone can learn, and we must all learn to deal with change quickly and effectively.

The Nature of Change

Most people are never taught how to deal effectively with change. There are no classes for it in school, no correspondence courses to take through the mail, and no corporate training programs. These kinds of courses would certainly be useful! Change 101 could teach people how to cope when life throws them an unexpected curve ball, such as divorce, illness, or bankruptcy. Change 102 could encourage people to proactively pursue positive changes in order to improve the quality of life, such as beginning a new career, fanning the flame of a smoldering marriage, or losing a few unhealthy pounds.

Change Is Universal

Changes, both good and bad, happen to everyone. As a matter of fact, the only thing that remains the same is change itself! Change is the essence of life; change is constant. We are constantly moving forward or going backward; there is no standing still.

Change Has a Scriptural Foundation

Do you realize that the Bible actually commands us to change? Not only does it command us to do this; it also tells us how. Romans 12:2 is a call-to-change scripture. The entire process of change can be encapsulated in this one verse. "And do not be conformed to this world, but be transformed by the renewing of your mind."

In the original language, the word *transformed* actually means changed. It is the word used to describe the metamorphosis of a caterpillar into a butterfly. The word *renew* also means to change. Given these definitions, the verse can be read like this: And do not be conformed to this world, but be changed by the changing of your mind.

The word transformed also implies a transition. Many people try to take one giant step to go from where they currently are to where they want to be. When they trip and fall, they cannot understand why. This is why we need to have a good understanding of the nature of change.

Change Is a Process

Many people view change as something that happens in a moment, but the truth is that change is a process. Just as a baby does not turn into a teenager overnight, change does not just happen. A baby must go through certain developmental stages in order to grow and mature, and in the same manner, we must progress through various stages of change in order for change to take root. At times these stages of change may seem to happen almost instantaneously, such as when a person is born-again, but they do happen.

....

Maybe the change you want is something relatively minor, such as the need to start getting to work on time! Or perhaps it is something more serious, such as the need to rewrite your marriage. Whatever changes you desire, understanding the process of change and the characteristics of each stage of change can assist you in making it through the transition.

The most difficult thing about change is that it deals with the unknown. Not knowing how things are going to turn out makes us uncomfortable! This feeling can lead us to respond in ways that are actually worse than the change itself.

I have seen people who have been fired or laid off from a job allow fear to absolutely overwhelm them. They just do not know what to do. Fear paralyzes them, and they get stuck. Once they overcome this fear and respond correctly by pursuing another business opportunity or by choosing another career, they usually end up doing much better at the new job than they did at the first one. What they feared in adjusting to their new circumstances was unfounded.

Two Types of Change

Forced Change

In the spring of 1998 in Jonesboro, Arkansas, a thirteen-year-old boy opened fire on his classmates. Apparently, the thing that motivated his assault was the fact that his girlfriend broke up with him the day before! He took guns to school and killed several innocent classmates because a change that he did not like was forced upon him.

We have all experience forced change like this boy did. Forced changes are external events that you did not initiate. They are changes that you did not choose and would rather not have. Look through this list below and see how many of these forced changes have ever touched your life:

- An illness
- A divorce
- A child on drugs

- A corporate downsizing
- The placement of an elderly parent in a nursing home
- A weather-related disaster
- A decrease in income or financial ability
- The death of a friend or family member
- An accident

Many people have tremendous difficulty coping with forced change. When the thirteen-year-old girl told her boyfriend that she didn't like him anymore, he experienced a forced change. Something happened that he did not want to happen, and he did not know how to deal with it constructively.

One reason that people have such a hard time with forced changes is that it is impossible to be prepared for them. When your boss says, "We are downsizing, and we do not need you anymore," it is usually a surprise. When your spouse announces, "I do not love you anymore; I want a divorce," you are usually caught off guard. The fact that the change is unexpected and unwanted makes it harder to accept.

Forced change is unsettling.

In more than twenty years of pastoring, I have seen many business people get transferred on their jobs and have to relocate to another city. Many times such a transfer was the result of a promotion, and a significant pay increase accompanied the move. Yet after a few months, many have called me and said, "Pastor, it is not like I expected. I thought I would find a church, make new friends, and enjoy my new environment, but this move has been tough! My kids are not adjusting well, and now even my wife and I are fighting." Forced change throws you off balance. It interrupts your life.

Forced change does not come to you as an isolated event.

When any change comes into your life, it effects more than one thing. When people relocate, for example, not only does their work environment change, but so does their home, their personal relationships, their church family, and even the weather around them. Many times people have a hard time handling change because it seems to strike in so many places at once! I have often heard people say in reference to a certain event, "It changed everything." Many times that is not an exaggeration. One change can affect everything.

Proactive Change

Some changes are not forced upon us but are ones we choose to make. These are proactive changes, and we make them because we desire to improve the quality of our lives. These changes involve internal rather than external events. The light dawns, and a middle-age man realizes that if he does not lose those extra hundred pounds, he may not live to see his grandchildren. A single mother decides to go back to college to further her education and her paycheck. Such changes are not forced upon you but rather are initiated by you.

Proactive change is invigorating.

There is something energizing about initiating a positive change in your life. It is exciting and fulfilling. The progress you make and the results you reap are highly beneficial. Whether it is overcoming a bad habit or adding some new friends to your social circle, the things that happen as a result of proactive change improve the quality of your life.

Proactive change is encompassing.

Just as forced change is not an isolated event, neither is proactive change. When you make an improvement in one area of your life, the change tends to have an effect on other areas as well. The man who begins and sticks to a morning workout regimen begins to feel better about himself and goes into the office in a happier mood. After several weeks, the boss notices his change in attitude and gives him a raise. The raise gives his wife and him extra money to go out on a weekly date, which improves their relationship. Because Mom and Dad are getting along better, the children of the family now feel more secure. Such is the domino effect of chosen change. A little goes a long way.

Emotional Effects of Change

When you experience any change, forced or proactive, you will first feel loss. Loss does not feel good! If you lose your job, you feel the loss of your paycheck and perhaps the loss of your feelings of dignity and self-worth. If you begin a diet, you feel the loss of being able to indulge in your favorite fattening foods. With every change, good or bad, there is a price to pay.

Change may also bring feelings of conflict. Conflict shows up primarily as anger. You feel like lashing out at someone, even God! You must be careful not to let this anger paralyze you. Some people are angry twenty years after the fact, and this anger immobilizes them so that they cannot make progress in life. A good way to channel your anger is to ask yourself, "What actions can I take right now that will enable me to successfully overcome this?" Anger can actually help propel you to the answers you need.

Another emotion you may feel during change is rejection. You feel life is against you or has not treated you fairly. You may think, "If the God of the universe really cared about me, I would not be experiencing this." You may feel as if no one has ever gone through the pain and suffering that you are going through and as if no one really understands.

Feelings such as these may leave you identifying with your loss. Many people begin to identify themselves by their problems or by their failures, but you are neither a problem nor a failure. Problems and failures are simply experiences that occur in your life; they are not you. Just as the label on a product is not the actual product, you are not your problems or failures.

I knew a woman who experienced tragedy with her three-year-old son. He escaped her attention for a few minutes and wandered down their short driveway into the street, where he was struck and killed instantly by an oncoming car. Due to this event, this woman labeled herself an unfit mother and became so overcome with guilt that she is still unable to function in society. When unwanted change comes, you must not see yourself as permanently connected to it.

The problem will go away. The failure will be forgotten. You will remain. One man eloquently stated, "There are vast undamaged areas in every human life if only we would discover them."

When you begin to identify yourself by your problems, you develop a victim's mentality. Victims are always asking "Why me?" Unfortunately, there is not always a reason. People who see themselves as victims in their situations have a strong tendency to lash out verbally, emotionally, or even physically at those they perceive as causing the injury. People who see themselves as victims may even lash out at those who are innocent but happen to be nearby! You may have heard it said that "hurting people hurt people." Too often this proves to be true.

Responses to Change

First Kings 3 tells the story of two women who had to deal with change. One of them had lost her baby. She rolled over on him in the middle of the night and suffocated him. Instead of dealing with her mistake, she took another woman's baby, put it beside her in bed, and left the dead baby at the other woman's side.

Change came to both these women in an instant. In the short time between going to bed and awakening, change hit them right between the eyes. One woman lost her son to death, and the other lost her son to a thief! Both experienced a forced change that they did not desire. Their responses, however, were very different.

When the women arrived before King Solomon, he offered a unique solution. He said to divide the living child in two and to give half the baby to each mother. The real mother protested, saying it would be better to give her child to the thief than to lose him to death. By this, King Solomon discerned which was the real mother, and the child was returned to her without harm.

These two women responded to change in an opposite manner. The one who lost her son to death developed a victim's mentality and struck out to injure an innocent party rather than work constructively through her loss. She put herself and her feelings in the center of the situation and probably asked herself, "Why me? Why not her?" She looked for a solution that would make her feel better in the short run and stole the other mother's baby. Her purpose was to make her pain stop immediately. She projected her problem onto the mother with the living son. As long as you are overwhelmed with change, you cannot deal with it objectively.

The mother of the living son also had change forced upon her. She went to bed the night before happy and content with her newborn, and she woke up with someone else's dead baby beside her! This mother could have lashed out in anger at the injustice. She could have even lashed out physically by trying to remove her son from the other woman's arms. Instead, she realized the situation was out of her control. Instead of centering on her pain, she looked for a constructive way to deal with the matter by submitting her problem to the king. When the king threatened to cut the baby in half, she still refused to focus on herself and her pain, but she focused on what was best for the child. Even though something terrible was happening to the most precious thing in her life, she remained objective enough to respond correctly. She was experiencing tremendous personal pain, yet she did not allow it to keep her from effectively coping with the forced change.

Everyone experiences forced change, but only people who choose to go through it correctly make good choices. Positive, healthy results are not produced unless you make the right choices. When you go through change correctly, personal growth takes place. The real mother in this story not only made the right choice on behalf of her child but also made the right choice on behalf of herself, and she got her baby back as a result!

You cannot look at life through lenses of self-pity or despondency and expect to deal with change constructively. To effectively deal with forced change, you must choose to have a positive response. You must be willing to personally grow to meet the challenge that negative change brings. When you choose to have the right perspective and to act on the right choices, you can emerge the winner in every situation. Even if your boss fires you unjustly, you can say, "I am going to use this change as a catalyst to propel me on to something bigger and better!"

Forced change is unsettling, but handling it correctly is invigorating. Forced change can become an opportunity clock rather than an alarm clock. By choosing your response, you can turn every situation to your personal advantage, regardless of the outward circumstances. I never sit around depressed, worrying about what changes are going to happen to me. I choose to stay excited about the new directions in which I am taking in my life.

Choosing Your Response

Your initial response to forced change should be, "I can swallow this."

When I was a young boy, my mother made me take cod liver oil. She would literally hold my nose and put the spoon in my mouth. Still I was the one who had to swallow it! That was not easy. I always had to have something to drink immediately afterward to get that nasty taste out of my mouth.

Swallowing forced change is the same way. We say, "It stinks!" Yet ultimately we must surrender to it if we are going to go on. Why is this? Because there is absolutely nothing we can do about it! We have to just accept it. Remember the old TV Westerns in which the good guys would wave a white flag and surrender to their enemies? The good guys would then be caught and thrown in prison. It always looked like as if it were over for the heroes, yet it was always from this prison that they would effect their way of escape. By the same token, we must surrender to forced change before we can escape its negative effects. No matter how bad the situation is, we must accept it before we can move on.

Some people refuse to swallow change and try instead to compromise with it. Instead of accepting it, they merely put up with it and resign themselves to minimizing its effect on life. They do not grow through change, but they grow around it. Take, for instance, what can happen to a rejected wife who suffers an unwanted divorce. She may go on with her social life, dating or even marrying another man, but still keep part of her heart reserved due to the risk of being hurt again. She has compromised with the change rather than accept it. She has allowed the unwanted change to capture part of her dignity and to damage her self-worth. Accepting the divorce in spite of the hurt and pain would free her to work through the negative emotions and to continue to grow.

••

Another response people give to change is to just endure it. When enduring, people fight change on the inside by simply waiting for things to change back to the old way. Enduring puts people in a defensive position rather than an offensive one. Their theory is that in time all will pass and return to normal; therefore, they take no proactive action in their circumstances. They believe they can outlast the change. Of course, the truth is that it is impossible to go through change totally unaffected. Taking a defensive stance only puts a person in a position to become bitter, not better. If a ball team stays on defense all the time, it grows tired and weary and is unable to score any points in the game. In the same manner, it is a deception for you to believe you can simply outlast change without being touched by it.

Resisting or avoiding change occurs when a person denies that a change has even occurred or admits that it has occurred but ignores its effects. Some people resist the death of a loved one by refusing to clear out any of the dead person's belongings and by continuing to talk about the person as if he or she were alive, even though the death occurred years earlier! If a tornado destroys your house and you resist it by saying it did not happen, the fact remains that it did happen, and your house is gone! Until you accept this fact, you will not take any positive action toward rebuilding.

Similarly, married couples may avoid each other after a fight by acting like the other person is not even in the room. By avoiding the change, they put off the inevitable event of having to resolve the original source of conflict. The best course of action in any negative situation is to face the situation squarely and then choose your best response.

Advice for Dealing with Change

Here are some positive things you can do when dealing with change:

1. Acknowledge that the change really happened. You cannot even begin to deal effectively with change until you have acknowledged it.

2.   Evaluate the change. Take the time to ask yourself some questions about what caused the change to come into your life. Consider some of the questions from the following list.

- Is this change just a result of living in an imperfect world? (Stuff really does just happen!)
- Is it a result of my personal choices and behavior?
- Is it a result of someone else's behavior and choices?
- Am I in an age transition (mid-life crisis or empty-nest syndrome)?
- Am I in a different age or era economically or socially? (Technology has caused change to happen suddenly in all of these areas and has affected how people live, work, and play.)
- If things are changing around me, am I keeping up?

3.   Do something! You must do something to manage the change you are experiencing. Change can make you feel as if your life is in a crisis. Interestingly, the Chinese word for crisis consists of two symbols: one that means trouble and one that means opportunity. Any change can mean either trouble or opportunity, depending on the actions you take to deal with it.

4.   Finally, you should include the change as a part of your life and use it as a steppingstone for your personal growth. Get through it, get what you can out of it, and get on with it! You are now ready to use this experience as a reference point to know how to deal with other changes that come your way.

A Word of Exhortation

The young boy in Jonesboro, Arkansas, chose to resist an unwanted change. If he had followed the advice in this chapter, he would have gone home and told his mother, "My girlfriend broke up with me, and it hurts." He would have asked himself appropriate questions that would have promoted personal growth: Why did she break up with me? Is there anything in my personality I need to change? Did I treat her with honor and respect? He would have decided on a course of action, finding another girlfriend or improving his social skills with his friends in general. Finally, he would have included the change as part of his life experience and moved on. Instead, this boy resisted change and reacted in a way that negatively altered his life and the lives of those around him forever.

A reporter interviewed a man in Maine who was 103 years old. The reporter said to him, "Sir, in 103 years you have seen multitudes of changes."

"Yes," the man replied, "and I've been against every one of them!"

Do not resist change! Remember that it is the only thing in your life that is going to remain constant. Instead, learn the process of change. Understanding where you are in the process of change will go a long way toward helping you manage the changes that come into your life. No matter what change comes upon you, say to yourself, "I believe I am wondrously made by God, and He has given me the capacity and the gifts to deal with this change correctly and to take my personal growth to the next level." You can change. Yes, you can!

The One Thing That Remains the Same— Change!

Summary

- Remember that only one thing remains the same—change!

- Change is universal; it happens to everyone.

- The Bible actually commands you to change (Romans 12:2).

- Change is a process that happens over time in stages.

- There are two types of change: forced and proactive. Forced changes come when external events that you do not initiate happen to you. Proactive changes are changes you choose to make to improve the quality of your life.

- In the process of change, you may feel loss, conflict, and rejection.

- Avoid identifying with your loss; you are not your problems.

- Avoid developing a victim's mentality. You may not be able to control the circumstances, but you can always control your responses.

- To deal effectively with change, you must acknowledge it, evaluate the reasons for it, do something about it, and use it as a catalyst to propel you to something bigger and better.

Epilogue

I encourage you today to make a decision to change your life by changing your mind. The principles in this book have helped me discover and fulfill so many things that I would otherwise have thought to be impossible.

You *will* change. The questions is *how* you will do it. Will you take the circumstances of life as they come and be forced to change unwillingly, or will you develop a strategy to meet change head-on and allow it to propel you to an exciting future?

I challenge you to move out of your comfort zone and discover the process of change. I believe you will uncover the untapped potential that lies within, enabling you to accomplish much more than you ever dreamed possbile. The major key to your better future is *you*!

For Additional Materials

  Correct Change Required is also available in a six-tape audio series. When ordering, please request tape series #CH06. You may contact author Bill Epperhart at

6500 W. Coal Mine Avenue
Littleton, Colorado 80123

Or you can call us at 1-888-832-0765. You may also contact us by email at tccdenver@aol.com.